Mary Cassatt: a Life in the Arts

As a young woman growing up in nineteenth-century America, Mary Stevenson Cassatt (1844-1926) made a bold decision. Rather than pursue the preferred path for women of her generation—matrimony and motherhood—she chose to become an artist. Cassatt saw her career as more than that of a typical "lady painter"; she sought the success, recognition, and financial reward that would make her the professional equal of a man. Through disciplined talent, determination, and a fiercely independent spirit, she turned her youthful dreams into reality, winning international notice and critical acclaim. Although she lived an extraordinary life for a woman of her time, she celebrated the quiet domesticity of other women's lives in her art. More than any other artist in the modern era, she reflected the world of women with genuine respect, presenting their daily experiences in the home, with their friends, and with their children as rich, rewarding, and worthwhile.

Born on May 22, 1844, in Allegheny City, Pennsylvania, Cassatt enjoyed a privileged childhood in an affluent and upwardly mobile family. Her parents, Robert Simpson and Katherine Kelso Cassatt, provided their five children—Lydia, Alexander (called Aleck), Robert, Mary, and Joseph (known by his middle name Gardner) with every possible advantage within their means. They also instilled in them a devotion to education

Pennsylvania Academy Modeling Class (1862)
When Cassatt enrolled at the Pennsylvania Academy of the Fine Arts in 1860, thirty percent of the students were women. All classes were open to them except those that employed nude models. This prohibition was lifted in 1868. There was great camaraderie between the women students. Elizabeth Haldeman wrote to her mother that when an inexperienced classmate was asked by a friend to make a cast of his hand, she and Cassatt helped her. Dr. Edmund Smith, the model, had this photograph taken to commemorate the event. Cassatt is on the far right, with Haldeman on the left.

Self-Portrait (1878)
Cassatt seldom used her own image in her work. In this rare self-portrait in gouache —an opaque watercolor—she appears as a genteel woman, dressed in a ruffled summer gown and a poke bonnet trimmed with flowers. Her delicate costume contrasts with her serious expression and intense gaze, reminding the viewer of her determined spirit. The light palette and free handling of the paint reveals the changes brought to her art by her association with the innovative circle of Impressionists.

and a pride in their father's Huguenot ancestry. A sense of restlessness also shaped the Cassatt family life. As an investment banker, Robert Cassatt constantly sought advancement, moving the household to a variety of cities in Pennsylvania throughout Cassatt's youth.

The family settled briefly in Philadelphia in 1849, but in the following year they all embarked on an extended visit to Europe. Like many Americans, Cassatt's parents regarded firsthand knowledge of European culture as a distinct educational advantage, but they were also seeking better medical care for their son Robert, who was in fragile health. Their tour included prolonged stays in Darmstadt, Heidelberg, and Paris, where the children were enrolled in school. Here young Mary demonstrated her natural gift for languages, easily acquiring German and French.

Little is known of the Cassatts' exact European itinerary, but given the family beliefs in education and opportunity, there is no doubt that they would have taken in all the sights and special events, such as the spectacular Exposition Universelle in Paris in 1855. The trip came to a tragic end in the summer of that year, when young Robert died in Darmstadt and the family headed home to Philadelphia.

Five years later, Cassatt began her education as an artist, enrolling as a full-time student at the Pennsylvania Academy of the Fine Arts. Renowned as a progressive institution, its whole curriculum—with the exception of classes employing nude models—was open to women. Preliminary training lasted for two years; before students were allowed to attempt painting or sculpture, they copied antique casts from the Academy's collection, attended anatomy lectures at the Penn Medical University, and, if they were male students, drew from live models.

But the Academy was more than an art school. With its strong collection and annual exhibition of Old Master works and new European paintings, it acquainted students with a wide range of both traditional and contemporary art. Cassatt, like many of the students, used the Academy's galleries as her classroom, escaping there to add variety to a regime she came to regard as stifling. In later years she dismissed the importance of the Academy's training on her own development as an artist. "Museums," she said, "are all the teachers one needs."

Despite the rich resources and progressive policies of the Academy, Cassatt set her sights higher. She was determined to go to Paris. Since the fall of Napoleon in 1815, the city reigned supreme as the art capital of the world. The teaching at the prestigious Ecole des Beaux-Arts was seen as unparalleled, and art students from the rest of Europe and the United States competed to enroll. Those who were not accepted sought private instruction in the studios of prominent painters, many of whom taught at the Ecole. The vast collections of the Louvre marked another opportunity for study, and young Americans, ardently copying the Old Masters, were a common sight in the galleries. Most aspiring artists had a single goal: to have a work accepted for the annual Salon, the elite showcase for contemporary talent, the first step on the path to recognition as an artist and a lucrative career.

In pursuit of her plan to get to Paris, Cassatt had to deal with several obstacles. First, during the Civil War (1861–5), the United States government imposed restrictions on European travel. Cassatt was forced to delay her trip until December 1865, six months after peace was concluded. Second, it would appear improper if she traveled alone, so she persuaded Eliza Haldeman, a classmate from the Academy, to meet her in Paris. Third, and most significantly, women

After Winslow Homer, **Art Students and Copyists in the Louvre Gallery, Paris** (1868)
In the nineteenth century, Paris was the art capital of the world. While students from Europe and the United States came to train with prominent painters, they also learned by making copies of the renowned works of art in the Louvre. This was a particularly popular practice among women, who were barred from the classes at the Ecole des Beaux-Arts. Cassatt believed in it, claiming that museums were "all the teachers one needs."

were not allowed to study at the Ecole, so Cassatt sought private instruction from one of its most influential professors, the painter Jean-Léon Gérôme.

Once in Paris, Cassatt and Haldeman took full advantage of all that the Parisian art world had to offer. They acquired licenses to copy in the Louvre, attended the classes for women in the studio of Charles Chaplin, and, in the summer, left the city to paint in the countryside. They enjoyed the freedom and ease of country life, and after a brief stay in Courances, southwest of Paris, settled in Ecouen, just ten miles (sixteen kilometers) north of Paris.

By 1867, the young women felt confident enough to enter works for the Salon—only to be rejected. But success came in the following year for both, with Cassatt exhibiting a portrait of a peasant woman in traditional costume called *La Mandoline*. On this occasion she used the name Mary Stevenson, to avoid, as Haldeman explained, "publicity" which might be unwelcome to a young lady living abroad and alone. The two women returned to Paris for the duration of the Salon, taking in the fashionable Parisian art scene and mixing with the stars of the official art world. But Haldeman noted that Cassatt seemed restless and eager to leave Paris.

Later that year, Cassatt moved back to the country, to Villiers-Le-Bel, northwest of Paris, where Thomas Couture, once a central figure in the Paris Salon and the Ecole (he had been Edouard Manet's teacher), now worked in seclusion. Haldeman joined Cassatt for a while, but then returned to Philadelphia, swapping artistic ambition for marriage and family.

Cassatt remained in Europe, going on a sketching tour in the Alps, then journeying on to meet her mother in Rome. In 1870 a work painted in Italy, *Contadina di Fabello; val Sesia (Piedmont)* was accepted by the Salon; this time she exhibited under her full name. But, as she noticed that the more advanced and controversial painters—Edouard Manet, Edgar Degas, Paul Cézanne—were often excluded from the Salon, her admiration for it waned. By August of that year, in the shadow of the Franco-Prussian war, she returned to her home in Pennsylvania, with plans to launch her professional career.

Her family, then residing in Altoona, soon moved back to Philadelphia, and there, in 1871, she opened her own studio. Late in life she claimed that her father discouraged her ambitions—declaring "I would almost rather see you dead"—but there is no evidence for it. On the contrary, her parents gave her full financial support, requiring only that she cover her own professional expenses.

By summer of that year, when her family moved to Hollidaysburg near Altoona to advance her brother Aleck's career with the Pennsylvania Railroad, she closed her studio. Stifled in this small town, Cassatt took her works to Pittsburgh and Chicago, looking for buyers. In Chicago, she narrowly escaped the fire of October 8, 1871, that destroyed the city—and her paintings. She was left with only her baggage. Frustrated and deeply disappointed, she longed to return to Europe, but could not afford the trip. A chance meeting with the bishop of Pittsburgh brought her a change of luck. Wanting some new embellishments for his cathedral, he commissioned Cassatt to copy two works in Parma by the sixteenth-century master Correggio. Cassatt quickly enlisted her friend the engraver Emily Sartain to join her. By December 1871, she had returned to Europe.

Cassatt and Sartain settled in Parma where their presence stirred considerable excitement, for young American art students rarely visited the town. With Cassatt's fluent Italian, probably picked up during her travels there in 1870, the women were readily accepted at the Accademia, where they received great encouragement. Cassatt managed to complete one of the Correggio copies, that of the *Coronation of the Virgin*, but her progress on the other is undocumented.

Now she turned her attention to local subjects. In 1872, she successfully placed one of her new paintings, *At the Carnival*, in the Paris Salon and became an overnight success. One American newspaper reported: "Miss Mary Stevenson Cassatt has just finished an original painting which all Parma is flocking to see...Italian painters of reputation are quite enthusiastic in regard to our fair young countrywoman's talent which they pronounce to be nearly akin to genius and they offer her every inducement to make Parma her home."

But Cassatt again became restless. Sartain left Parma for Paris, while in that autumn Cassatt made a journey to Spain, visiting Madrid and settling for a while in Seville. Here she experimented with a darker, more dramatic palette and Spanish subjects; her depiction of a *Torero and Young Girl* was accepted for the 1873 Salon. That summer, in her mother's company, she visited Holland and Belgium, and after her mother's departure in the fall, she briefly returned to Parma and Rome. She concluded her travels in 1874, when she again rented an apartment in Paris. Here she was joined by her older sister Lydia, who willingly took upon herself the task of organizing the domestic details of Cassatt's life.

Determined to secure a position in the art world of Paris, Cassatt first chose a conventional path—painting portraits of Americans abroad. She also submitted a work to the Salon of 1875, hoping this would bring her good publicity. But, to her embarrassment, the work—now lost, it was believed to be a full-length study of her sister Lydia—was rejected. After her repeated successes of previous years, Cassatt saw this decision as arbitrary and now viewed the judgments of the Salon jury with increasing skepticism.

Always passionate about the arts, she held strong opinions. In 1873, Emily Sartain had written to her father that while she enjoyed discussing art with her friend, they often disagreed. Cassatt was "entirely too slashing," but, Sartain acknowledged that Cassatt's views revealed "the earnestness with which she loves her profession." Over the years, Cassatt's taste had changed, and she now felt that the luminaries of the Salon—Alexandre Cabanel, Léon Bonnat, and even Jean-Léon Gérôme—paled by comparison with the Old Masters.

Meanwhile, Cassatt received visitors in her Paris apartment, many of them independent-minded American women interested in the arts. Her circle

included May Alcott, the sister of novelist Louisa May Alcott, who described her hostess as a "woman of real genius." Alcott predicted that Cassatt would be "a first-class light as soon as her pictures get a little circulated and known, for they are handled in a masterly way, with a touch of strength one seldom finds coming from a woman's fingers."

As in Parma and Seville, Cassatt found her subjects in the life around her, but now the emphasis was more on the world of women. She depicted her visitors at tea, her sister absorbed in needlework or reading, an elegant friend dressed to appear in public. Her portrayal of modern life had a natural sense of immediacy that allied her with that most progressive of all the independent artistic circles—the group popularly known as the Impressionists.

In April 1874, a small group of artists, including Claude Monet, Pierre Auguste Renoir, Edgar Degas, and Alfred Sisley, had chosen to vent their frustration at the repeated rejections of their work by the Salon jury by holding their own exhibition. They called themselves the "Société anonyme des artistes peintres, sculpteurs, graveurs." When the critic Louis Leroy dismissed Monet's *Impression: Soleil levant* as "only an impression," rather than a finished work, the public came to know them by the term "Impressionists." The artists in the group embodied a spirit of independence, working in distinct styles and united more by an interest in modern subjects and natural composition than by any aesthetic preferences. While Cassatt never mentioned in her

Mary Cassatt (c. 1872)
Cassatt traveled to Parma with her friend the engraver Emily Sartain in the early months of 1872. Sartain left the city in the Spring to study painting in Paris. This carte-de-visite *of Cassatt is inscribed "To the distinguished painter Emily Sartain," to encourage her friend's new endeavor. In contrast to the typically serious demeanor associated with photographic portraiture of the time, Cassatt appears friendly, even flirtatious. She enjoyed her stay in Parma where she achieved her first public success.*

The Bacchante (1872)
Cassatt's admiration for Old Master paintings is recorded in her early experimental styles. In The Bacchante, painted during her stay in Parma, her golden palette reveals a deep response to sixteenth-century Italian painting. Although she selected a subject popular with academic painters, she sought a sense of realism, choosing the model for her "splendid head like a Roman," and depicting her in the traditional costume of Parma. When Cassatt traveled to Spain in the following year, she painted in darker tones, with black shadows and red accents, the same palette used by Baroque masters such as Velazquez.

correspondence that she had attended any of the Société's exhibitions, she must surely have been aware of them and clearly would have felt an affinity with their daring aims and unorthodox pictures.

In 1877, after experiencing a further rejection from the Salon, Cassatt received a visit from Edgar Degas. He expressed a long-held sympathy with her work; her Salon picture of 1874, *Ida*, had prompted him to declare "Here is someone who feels as I do." Cassatt had admired Degas's work since 1873, when her excitement at seeing a selection of his pastels in a picture dealer's shop prompted her to "flatten my nose against that window" to "absorb all I could." Degas urged her to exhibit with the Impressionists. She accepted without hesitation, and regarded it as the turning point in her life and in her art: "I accepted with joy. I hated conventional art. I began to live."

Cassatt's debut with the Impressionist group came in the spring of 1879. She presented eleven works— in paint and pastel—and, despite the derogatory reviews that the group continued to receive from the conservative art press, her pieces were well received. Her command of harmonious color and the gentility of her modern life subjects won praise. The critic for *L'Artiste* observed "There is nothing more graciously honest and aristocratic than her portraits of young women." She exhibited with the group a further three times—in 1880, 1881, and 1886—always to favorable reviews. Although not the only woman in the group— Berthe Morisot, Eva Gonzales, and Marie Bracquemond were also among them—Cassatt was the only American.

Participation in the Impressionist exhibitions brought a public interested in advanced art. Now Cassatt could pursue her career on her own terms, and, by 1881, she had secured the services of a dealer, Paul Durand-Ruel, who also represented other Impressionist painters. With the confidence that comes from the support of like-minded colleagues, strong reviews, and ever-increasing sales, Cassatt unleashed her desire to experiment, using a freer brush stroke, a more luminous palette, and a greater sense of natural accident in her compositions.

Cassatt and Degas forged a close and enduring friendship, but their relationship was volatile. Both were highly opinionated, and their arguments occasionally led to what Cassatt's friend Louisine Elder (later Havemeyer) called "spicy estrangements." Degas's judgments were often caustic, but Cassatt valued his praise above all other. For his part, he enjoyed working with her, and in 1879 persuaded her to produce some etchings for a new journal he was planning to publish, *Le Jour et La Nuit*.

Bringing together images of and articles about contemporary life, Degas intended his publication to celebrate the modern point of view. He also hoped it would produce a steady income. Cassatt appeared as a model in the etchings and pastels of the Louvre that he produced for it. In them he portrayed her as tall, willowy, and stylish—a knowing observer strolling through the galleries. Unfortunately, Degas's plans came to nothing, and the journal never appeared.

In 1877, after her father retired from business, he and Mrs. Cassatt joined their daughters in Paris.

Together they rented an apartment large enough to accommodate regular visits from their sons Aleck and Gardner, as well as their new daughters-in-law and their growing families. As before, Cassatt found her subjects for paintings in her surroundings, often portraying her mother and sister in their daily activities. In fact, her family was a great source of strength and inspiration. When her sister Lydia died of Bright's disease in November 1882, Cassatt was overwhelmed with grief. Months later, visiting from the United States, her sister-in-law Lois observed that "She has not had the heart to touch her painting for six months and will scarcely now be persuaded to begin."

But Cassatt returned to her work with new mastery and to new acclaim. In 1886, her pictures appeared in the first major exhibition of Impressionist art in the United States, organized by Durand-Ruel. Her nieces and nephews, who often visited from the States, now appeared regularly in her works, and in 1888 she depicted Gardner's wife Jennie with her infant son— the first dated example of the most enduring theme of her later career: the loving bond of mother and child.

The years also brought hardships that called her away from her work. Her mother's failing health was a source of constant worry, and her own health suffered in 1889 when a riding accident left her with a broken leg. Soon after her recovery, her father entered a physical and mental decline, and he required increasing care until his death in December 1891.

Meanwhile, the interest Cassatt had shown in printmaking while working with Degas continued. Now she tried her hand at drypoint. The demanding precision of this technique required skill, discipline, and complete attention. The challenge appealed to Cassatt, who explained: "*That* is what teaches one to draw. In drypoint you are down to the bare bones, you can't cheat." Twice in 1889 and 1890, at the Galerie Durand-Ruel, she exhibited her new prints alongside those of colleagues from the Impressionist circle as part of the Société des Peintres-Graveurs.

In May 1890, a major exhibition of Japanese color prints held at the Ecole des Beaux-Arts inspired Cassatt to take her own printmaking in a new direction. The woodblock images of late eighteenth- and early nineteenth-century masters of the *ukiyo-e* ("pictures of the floating world") such as Utamaro and Hokusai had been known in Paris since the opening of Japan to international trade in the mid-nineteenth century, but the scope of this exhibition, with over seven hundred prints organized by the collector Siegfried Bing, was unprecedented.

The subjects that featured intimate scenes of women's lives no doubt struck a chord with Cassatt, and she set herself the challenge of finding a counterpart in her own work. The result was a combination of drypoint—for the strong contour lines—and aquatint, in which a layer of resin creates graded tonal effects. Color was dabbed on the printing plate *à la poupée* with "dolls" made of rags. She shared her new enthusiasm with Berthe Morisot, one of the other women of the Impressionist group, urging her to see the exhibition: "You who want to make color prints you couldn't dream of anything more beautiful...You *must* see the Japanese—*come as*

LEFT Edgar Degas, **Portrait of Mary Cassatt** (c. 1884)
The force of Cassatt's personality shines through in this vivid oil portrait by her friend Degas. Leaning forward, as if to share a confidence, she gazes knowingly to one side. Cassatt, however, disliked this work, complaining that "It represents me as a person so repugnant that I do not want anyone to know I posed for it." She may have objected to the cards in her hand or her assertive—and indecorous—position. Although she had progressive views on the arts, she was often described as conservative and prim—strong evidence of the enduring influence of her middle-class American upbringing.

RIGHT Edgar Degas, **Visit to a Museum** (c. 1879-80)
This pastel of Cassatt and her sister Lydia in the galleries at the Louvre is one of several studies Degas made for the etched illustrations of the ill-fated journal Le Jour et La Nuit. *In it, Degas captures Cassatt's natural grace and style. Tall and slender, she enjoyed dressing in the newest fashions and wore them well. Her easy and confident demeanor suggests that the museum is her domain. This affectionate portrait is a tribute to her authority as well as to her elegance.*

Mother Louise Nursing her Child (1899)

Cassatt's interest in printmaking first appears in the etchings she made for Degas's journal Le Jour et La Nuit *in 1879. Over a decade later, she returned to printmaking, this time in highly experimental mode. She particularly liked drypoint. Unlike etching, it does not use any acid. Instead, the image is made by dragging a diamond-point needle across a copper plate, creating the grooves that contain the ink transferred to the paper. As in a sketch, Cassatt often left the figures unfinished. Here, just a few lines indicate Mother Louise's body and the disappearing contours of the baby's hands and feet.*

Reflection (c. 1890)

Drypoint challenged Cassatt to attain precision in her drawing. Whereas in pencil or chalk mistakes can be altered, drypoint does not allow the artist to "cheat." Cassatt used the technique to hone her drawing skills; she rarely made more than five or six impressions, and she pulled them herself. As seen in this example, Cassatt exploited to the full the distinct and calligraphic line produced by drypoint. This print has all the subtlety of her drawing.

soon as you can." Inspired by these images, Cassatt produced a series of ten color prints, all featuring scenes from a woman's day, including bathing, dressing, writing letters, and caring for children. They were shown at her first solo exhibition in April 1891 at Durand-Ruel's Parisian establishment, and were sold as a set in his New York gallery.

The first clear recognition of Cassatt in her homeland came through an invitation from Bertha Honoré Palmer, an arts patron and socialite, to paint a mural celebrating "The Modern Woman" for the Woman's Pavilion at the 1893 Columbian Exposition in Chicago. It was to appear with Mary Fairchild MacMonnie's "The Primitive Woman." The mural was so large that Cassatt found it necessary to build a special studio to accommodate it. The work— unlocated, perhaps destroyed—presented allegorical figures in contemporary dress: *Young Women Plucking Fruits of Knowledge* was the central subject, flanked by *Young Girls Pursuing Fame* and *Art, Music, Dancing.* Cassatt sent the completed work to Chicago, but did not see it installed. Although she showed no interest in working again on such a grand scale, the figure ensembles of the mural—women picking fruit and playing music— appeared in her work for the rest of her life.

Meanwhile, Cassatt's mother was becoming increasingly frail. Cassatt devoted as much time as possible to her, taking her to warm places in the winter as well as, in summer, to the country retreat which Cassatt had bought in 1894. This house— Château Mesnil-Beaufresne— stood fifty miles (eighty kilometers) northwest of Paris. After Katherine Cassatt's death in October 1895, Cassatt observed a brief period of mourning, but soon returned to her work, finding comfort in the familiar routine. For more than five years, she had been burdened with caring for her elderly parents. Her loss was great, but now she was free to put her own needs first. She took the opportunity to spend more time quietly working at Château Mesnil-Beaufresne, away from the noise and demands of Paris.

In 1898, Cassatt made her first journey back to the States for twenty-three years. She visited friends and family, as well as artists and collectors. She also painted a number of portraits, renewed her friendship with Louisine Havemeyer, and met the architect Theodate Pope, who became a valued friend in her later years. The *Philadelphia Ledger* announced her visit in a brief news item: "Mary Cassatt, sister of Mr. Cassatt, president of the Philadelphia Railroad, returned from Europe yesterday. She has been studying painting in France and owns the smallest Pekingese in the world." (She actually kept griffons.) Cassatt's response to this demeaning notice was never recorded, but it undoubtedly reminded her why she had needed to leave America to make her reputation. Only a few years earlier she had written to Bertha Palmer: "After all give me France—women do not have to fight for recognition here, if they do serious work." Cassatt returned to France that summer, traveling to the States only one more time, in 1908, on the occasion of the death of Havemeyer's husband.

Meanwhile, Cassatt continued to re-work and refine her vision of women at their daily chores. But who were these women? Many, like her mother and sister can be identified, but although their likenesses were often recognizable, Cassatt frequently generalized their features, so they appeared simply as anonymous women absorbed in their daily activities.

Cassatt also pressed friends, neighbors, and her household staff into posing for her, as well as employing professional models. Some sitters are identified by name—Susan, Mother Louise, Mother Jeanne. But their names and histories are of little consequence, for Cassatt was seeking to portray a universal rather than an individual experience of contemporary womanhood. It is as if, by showing those aspects of women's lives that were common to all, she wanted to convey the sisterhood of women.

The lives of those women had been shaped by the sweeping social changes of the mid-nineteenth century, especially in the United States. The decline of agricultural work and cottage industry brought the rise of the cities and a new affluence. Increasingly, the male head of the household worked outside of the home. Women, who in previous generations had helped their husbands in business by managing shops, supervising apprentices, and keeping the accounts, now directed their energies toward maintaining an ordered and pleasant home. These distinct roles—male breadwinner and female homemaker—put men and women in separate worlds. While men made their way in the public arena, women spent their time in the privacy of the home, organizing the household and its staff, cultivating the family friends, and nurturing the family's children. Although Cassatt

Mary Cassatt in Paris (c.1903)
Cassatt was widely admired for her strong opinions and keen intelligence. Young Americans studying abroad sought her out to ask for advice. The American artist and critic George Biddle described her as "one of the most vital, high-minded, dedicated, and prejudiced human beings I have ever known." The European press often attributed her fierce independence to her American origins. She always described herself as "definitely and frankly American." This photograph was taken by her friend Theodate Pope, who inscribed the verso "Mary Cassatt in Paris."

Mary Cassatt at Grasse
(1911)

Cassatt loved the country. As early as 1860, her family kept a rural residence in West Chester, Pennsylvania, as a summer retreat. During her student days in Paris, she preferred to live in small country towns, taking regular trips to the capital. After visiting Grasse, the French perfume-making town on the Riviera, she rented the Villa Angeletto there in November 1912 and remained there through the following year. Although she had traveled to the south of France to improve her health, her residence in Grasse led to a renewal of her friendship with the Impressionist artist Pierre Auguste Renoir.

herself struggled against the restrictions that defined women's lives, she recognized that those lives—in moments of solitude, in social exchange, in public appearance, and in intimate expression—possessed an inherent dignity and strength. As a result, her art offers us a sympathetic view of women at a time when their lives were very different from our own.

Cassatt's increasing artistic endeavor brought her even wider recognition and greater honors during the first decade of the new century. In 1904 she was awarded the Lippincott prize for her painting *The Caress*—her first work to be shown at the Pennsylvania Academy, and in the same year she was also offered an award from the Chicago Art Institute, but she declined them both. However, at the end of the year, she did accept the Légion d'Honneur from the French government. Another indication of her growing renown was recalled in 1910 by Ambroise Vollard, who had become her dealer in 1905. Vollard reported that she was once present—but not recognized—among a group of people discussing Impressionist painters. One man pointed out that they were neglecting a "foreign painter that Degas ranks very high." Cassatt inquired who he meant, and upon hearing her own name said: "Oh, nonsense!"

Increasingly, Cassatt devoted time to travel, acting as an art consultant for the Havemeyers on their collecting expeditions and joining her brother Gardner's family on a trip down the Nile in 1911. She continued to work, refining her now-favorite theme of maternal devotion. She also granted lengthy interviews to Achille Segard, who, in 1913, wrote the first biography of her—*Mary Cassatt: Un Peintre des enfants et des mères*. But a decline in her eyesight was diagnosed as cataracts, and for five years she endured a series of unsuccessful operations. Inevitably, this condition ended her career as an artist.

Although World War I made life even at her country residence difficult, she took pleasure in her continuing friendship with Havemeyer, who became active in the American Women's Suffrage Movement. Cassatt, too, supported women's rights, and in April 1915 she participated in the "Suffrage Loan Exhibition," organized by Havemeyer at Knoedler's Gallery in New York. The exhibition featured a selection of Old Master paintings, together with works by Degas and Cassatt. Although this was Cassatt's first public demonstration of her political beliefs, the fact that her work was hung alongside that of the Old Masters would have been at least as important to her as the political statement.

In the following years she lived quietly at Mesnil-Beaufresne. Despite her failed vision and increasing frailty, she remained fiercely independent, continuing to write her own letters until 1925 and making regular excursions in her chauffeur-driven car. When she died on June 14, 1926, she left as a legacy not only her art, but the example of her life, proving that a woman could be, in her own words, not "something" but "somebody." For the next five years, memorial exhibitions in France and the United States, commemorated her work—that respectful and dignified view of the lives of women, graced with subtle strength and genuine satisfaction.

Solitude

Whether absorbed in a book, attentive to their needlework, or deep in personal contemplation, the women in Mary Cassatt's art find contentment in their solitude. And, it is striking how frequently Cassatt depicted women on their own. Their poses and gestures define the boundaries of their privacy. They turn their back to the viewer or incline their heads, looking only at their work. Their faces, when not obscured by shadow, express their deep concentration. Moreover, by presenting her sitters so deeply involved in their work, Cassatt reminds the viewer to keep a respectful distance. Although these women engage in a variety of activities, they all share a sense of tranquil self-fulfillment. In her domestic setting, each woman seems at ease with herself, perfectly content to be left alone. Rather than a place for the confinement of women, Cassatt defines the home as a realm of personal endeavor, constructive work, and self-realization.

Lydia Crocheting in the Garden at Marly (1880)
In the summer of 1880, the Cassatt family rented a villa with a comfortable garden at Marly-le-Roi. Cassatt took the opportunity to experiment in plein-air painting. Lydia, her face shaded from the sun by a broad-brimmed bonnet, is warmly dressed in a blue coat. The dense green foliage and dull purple border plants behind her offer a subtle color contrast. Degas saw this oil painting, which appeared in the Impressionist exhibition of 1881, as evidence of Cassatt's artistic growth, noting that the work "looked well in studio light. It is much stronger and nobler than what she did last year."

The social changes of the nineteenth century—most notably among the rising urban middle class—gave women more time alone than previously. The professions of the affluent after the middle of the century—business, finance, administration—required men to work outside the home. With men absent, the house became a female domain.

The size of the household also decreased during the nineteenth century. In its early decades, several generations of a family, as well as distant relatives and non-relations, such as apprentices and boarders, shared one residence. But by the end of the century, the immediate family—mother, father, and children—occupied the home on their own. Even modest members of the middle class employed servants—usually a cook and a housemaid—freeing the woman of the house from the dull but necessary routine tasks of running a home. Increasingly, a middle-class woman's time was her own, to be filled as she saw fit.

As a professional artist, Cassatt knew the value of privacy and of having time to oneself. She often spent up to eight hours in her studio, preferring not to be interrupted. While her life as a working woman was unusual for her era, the lives of her sister and mother more closely followed convention. Cassatt could observe them in her own household as they filled their days with quiet yet constant activity.

A woman such as her mother or sister mostly spent her morning hours in solitude. With a gentle knock on the door, a servant would wake her, then quietly enter the bedroom with warm water for washing and a light breakfast, a cup of tea or coffee, and some bread or a biscuit. After putting down the breakfast tray and pouring the water in a pitcher, the servant would leave the room, allowing the woman to bathe in private. As seen in Cassatt's print *Woman Bathing*, a woman stood at a stand to wash, pouring the water from the pitcher into a basin. She would refresh her face, lightly sponge her body, and perhaps apply some toilet water and hand cream. After she had finished washing, she might summon her maid to help her dress, or if the costume was simple, she could dress unassisted.

A daytime or "morning" gown, was the plainest dress in a woman's wardrobe. Typically made of striped or printed cotton or dark-colored wool, the dress featured a high neck and long sleeves, with only modest decorative touches of ruffles or lace. In Cassatt's day, light corsets were worn even under these simple gowns; a maid's help was generally required to lace them. Many women also had the maid comb and dress their hair, twisting it up into a chignon that was secured with combs. Cassatt relied

Woman Bathing (1891)
This drypoint enhanced with aquatint demonstrates Cassatt's response to the ukiyo-e *tradition. The flattening of forms, the sliding perspective, and the contrast of decorative pattern and blank space reveal that Cassatt used the Japanese aesthetic as a point of departure. Even the subject suggests the intimacy of the art of the "floating world." This print is one of the "Set of Ten" that were shown in her first solo exhibition at the Galerie Durand-Ruel in 1891.*

**Lydia Seated in the Garden
with a Dog in her Lap**

(c. 1880)

*The setting of a spring garden, alive
with flowers, was often used by
nineteenth-century artists to enhance
the beauty of their female sitters, but
in this oil, Cassatt emphasizes a
woman's presence rather than her
appearance. Engrossed in her
needlework and with a little dog
resting comfortably in her lap, Lydia
Cassatt enjoys the warmth of the
sun, seated with her back to the
viewer. Her actions seem natural
rather than posed, and the contrast
of the cool colors of her costume
with the brightness of the blossoms
reveals Cassatt's adoption of the
fresh tones favored by the
Impressionists.*

on Mathilde, the head of her household staff, to do her hair and help her dress.

Once she had on her morning gown, a woman was ready to appear outside of her bedroom, but not outside her house. Many chose to remain alone for the whole morning, joining other members of the household only for the substantial late morning meal, when the social time of the day began. In Henry James's novel *Portrait of a Lady* (1881), young Isabel Archer admires the cultivated Madame Merle, whose "rigid possession of her morning" occupied her alone in her room until luncheon.

Domestic-related correspondence kept many women busy during the morning. Running the household required that she place orders for goods and pay the bills. In addition to attending to these affairs, the woman of the house coordinated the social life for all the family members, extending invitations, and accepting or rejecting social obligations. Personal correspondence also filled a

Girl Arranging Her Hair (1886)

Lost in thought, a young woman in an unadorned white shift runs her fingers through her hair. Like her garment, the modest room is simple and without decoration. By using a plain model and an everyday subject, Cassatt challenged her own ability to compose a picture and paint. It is believed that she painted this work to disprove Degas's chauvinistic dismissal that women knew nothing about "style." When Cassatt exhibited this oil at the final Impressionist exhibition, Degas gave it his highest endorsement, requesting that she give it to him in exchange for one of his. The picture remained in his collection to his death.

woman's time. Often letters provided the only link between friends and family living apart. Ranging from brief and informative to long and intimate, letters gave a woman the opportunity to share her experiences and, if the reader was an intimate confidant, her feelings.

Letter writing, like so many activities of the era, followed a strict decorum. "Form" books, such as Elizabeth Gaskell's *Compendium of Forms* (1882), offered examples of different types of letters, ranging from formal business correspondence to pleasant and chatty exchanges between friends. Gaskell stresses the "importance of perfect truthfulness" in personal or "domestic" letters, explaining that they reveal "a photograph of the inner life or character of the writer." She cautions never to answer correspondence while in a state of excitement or under duress, and urges a woman to ask herself "How will this look in a year or ten years hence?" But she encourages each writer to "open [her] heart to [her] friend in [her] letter," claiming that there is no better way for friends and relatives to "keep strong and bright the ties that bind" than honest and frequent correspondence.

Like many Americans residing abroad, Cassatt kept up a rich and lively exchange of letters with friends and family in the United States. During her student days, she used them to keep her family up-to-date and involved in her rising career, while later in life some of her closest friendships—those with Louisine Havemeyer and Theodate Pope—were maintained by mail. Using warm words to address female friends, in her letters Cassatt follows prevailing convention, opening one to Emily Sartain in 1871 with "Dear my Friend & Fellow Student" or closing a New Year's greeting to Havemeyer in 1902 as "ever affectionately" with "Lots of love to all." But, her correspondence also reveals her individuality. She uses foreign expressions—French, Italian, and Spanish—freely and, with close friends, she takes a teasing tone, peppering her language with slang. Her letters capture her personality— energetic, bright, and challenging. Whether she is writing to her brother Aleck of "Stott...a cheeky young English painter" or proudly informing Pope that her niece Eugenia has "bloomed like a rose," Cassatt's presence is vividly felt in her words.

A woman could also spend her solitary hours reading. By the middle of the century, most affluent women were educated, generally at home under the guidance of a governess or tutor. Fluency in a second language—usually French—was often one of the goals of female education. Although reading was widely accepted as a respectable pastime for a woman, what she read and the amount of time she devoted to reading was a subject of wide debate. In strict religious households, female readers limited themselves to books of moral instruction and the Bible. Novels and poems were strictly prohibited. Even in more liberal homes, too much attention to fiction—particularly novels in French—branded a woman as frivolous for wasting time on fantasy when she could be extending her grasp of history and culture. In some less cultured households, reading

during the day was discouraged. It was regarded as a lazy indulgence that distracted a woman from productive activities like needlework or organizing charity events and other philanthropic endeavors. But many women turned to books to fill their private time; like Henry James's Isabel Archer, motivated by genuine curiosity and an active imagination, a woman could transcend the limitations of her daily routine by reading: "To say she was so occupied is to say that her solitude did not press upon her."

The women in Cassatt's household were avid readers and highly intellectual. As a girl, Katherine Cassatt had studied with a French-educated tutor; in her own household she had high expectations of her daughters. Robert Cassatt was proud of his younger daughter's reputation as a keen-minded and intellectual woman. In 1878, he wrote to his son Aleck that she drew respect "among artists and literary people," not just for her powers as a painter, "but also for literary taste & knowledge & which moreover she deserves for she is uncommonly well read especially in French literature." Cassatt used the image of a woman engrossed in a book to en-dorse reading as a worthwhile female pursuit. This recurring theme links her first paintings of contem-porary Parisian life to her mature and late work.

It was a motif that had long endured in French art. In the middle years of the eighteenth century, artists such as Jean-Marc Nattier and François Boucher included books in portraits to impress the viewer with the wit and intelligence of the sitter. Later in the century, Jean Honoré Fragonard portrayed female

Reading Le Figaro

(1878)

Shortly after her parents joined her in Paris, Cassatt painted this portrait of her mother reading a French newspaper. The subject recalls Paul Cézanne's portrait of his father of 1866. Cassatt experiments with tone and composition, limiting her palette to whites and grays and including the reflection in a mirror. The painting was exhibited in New York City in 1879 at the Society of American Artists, where a critic, who described it as a "capitally-drawn figure of a middle-aged lady," praised Cassatt for demonstrating "how well an ordinary person dressed in an ordinary way can look."

LEFT **On the Balcony** (1878-9)
*Eighteenth-century French painters, such
as François Boucher and Jean Honoré
Fragonard, sometimes depicted women
reading. While the subject bore witness
to increasing literacy among women, it
also gave these male painters the
opportunity to present a pretty woman so
involved in something as to be unaware
of the presence of an appreciative male
spectator. Cassatt's interest was different.
Here, she offers a glimpse of everyday
life rather than a look at a woman with
the calculated gaze of a voyeur. The
fresh color, open-air setting, and the
sense of rapid execution give this lovely
oil painting a natural freshness, as if
the sitter will carry on with her other
activities as soon as she finishes reading
the newspaper.*

RIGHT **Woman Reading:
Portrait of Lydia Cassatt, the
Artist's Sister** (1878-9)
*The blunt-nosed profile and the curly
tendrils of hair tumbling over her
forehead distinguish this sitter as Lydia
Cassatt. But, by casting a shadow over
the face and placing the body at a
slight angle, Cassatt puts the emphasis
on the woman's act of reading the
morning paper rather than her identity.
With a loosely defined background, the
artist creates a solitary space that is
appropriate to a woman engrossed in
her reading.*

readers as pert, pretty, and desirable. Their intense concentration made them oblivious to the appreciative gazes of men. Cassatt gave this tradition a modern—and even feminist—twist by depicting many of her sitters reading newspapers. In the portrait of her mother *Reading Le Figaro* (page 33), the French-language journal is doubly significant. Painted shortly after her parents settled in with her in Paris, the journal is evidence of Katherine Cassatt's sharp interest in the political and intellectual world of her new country of residence. But, since a number of Impressionist portraits also feature the sitter reading a newspaper, it also indicates Cassatt's artistic affiliations with Impressionism. In *Reading Le Figaro*, as well as in similar works such as *Woman Reading: Portrait of Lydia Cassatt, the Artist's Sister* (page 35), the act of reading is focused, immediate, and genuine. Neither flattering nor provocative, these images are simply an honest glimpse of intelligent women who read not only to pass the time, but to keep their knowledge of the world up to date.

Another way for a woman to fill her time productively was to turn to needlework, some forms of which were regarded as an artistic hobby. Although a substantial number of middle-class women still made their clothing at home, the more affluent ordered their wardrobes from established dressmakers. Women of more modest means often hired seamstresses or bought their clothing ready-made from the new department stores. The needle crafts practiced as pastimes produced decorative and personal items—gifts, infant layettes, and trimmings for linen and lingerie. In addition, there were always things that needed repair, but in wealthy homes, servants saw to the mending.

The most popular decorative sewing technique was Berlin work. Carried out on a frame or a hoop, it was characterized by a variety of counted-thread stitches and colorful wool. Similar to present-day needlepoint or *petit point*, Berlin work was used to create scenic pictures and to embellish more practical items such as cushions, firescreens, and protective slipcases for shoes. Although young women were discouraged from giving expensive presents to their male friends, they could show off their skills with a modest, hand-made gift of an eyeglass case or a watch fob.

In the painting *Lydia at a Tapestry Frame* (pages 37-8), Cassatt portrays her sister busy at this craft. Although Bright's disease, an inflammatory condition of the kidneys which proved fatal, drained her energy and ill-health often confined her to the house, Lydia's capable hands were rarely still. She was skilled at all the needle arts, and her decorative work added a

Young Woman Working in a Garden (c. 1880-2)
Total absorption in what they are doing typifies Cassatt's depiction of women engaged in solitary work. It is hard to imagine distracting this young woman from her sewing. With her head down, her lips pressed tightly together, she works a piece of lace, perhaps a trimming for a collar or cuff. Cassatt emphasizes the intense concentration of her body, placing it so that it dominates the picture plane. The stable monumentality of the figure, painted in solid blocks of color and cool tones, is emphasized by the contrast of the loosely sketched trees and flowers and the bright geraniums.

special touch to even the most mundane items. But, not all women were as gifted. In Edith Wharton's *The Age of Innocence* (1920), May Archer's large hands, well-suited for her athletic endeavors, lack the requisite deftness. As a newly married woman, she struggles over her work, "laboriously stabbing the canvas" and, knowing that "other wives embroidered cushions for their husbands, she did not wish to omit this last link in her devotion."

Another type of needlework was white-on-white embroidery used to enhance more delicate items, such as fine linens, lingerie, and baby clothes. In Cassatt's painting *Woman Sewing* (1886), a youthful seamstress—perhaps her maid Susan—is engrossed in this type of fine work. Cutwork, and even light beading, added additional decorative touches. Elegant accessories, such as removable collars and cuffs, were embellished with cotton thread, tatted or crocheted in lacy patterns. These could be added to a plain dress for variety or to make it look new for another season. Women also crocheted or tatted

Lydia at a Tapestry Frame (c. 1881)
Decorative needlework, in multicolored wool worked on a frame in a variety of stitches, demanded skill and concentration. In this freely painted oil, Cassatt depicts her sister totally engaged in taxing work. The bold brush work and loose modeling of the shapes form an intriguing counterpoint to the precision of Lydia's movements. Her bright dress, patterned in rose and green, sets off her pale complexion. Soft, suffused light glimmers through the gauzy curtain; it is the only thing from outside to penetrate this quiet interior.

decorative edgings for petticoats, handkerchiefs, and lace or muslin fichus. Knitting was for practical items—shawls, bedjackets, stockings, mufflers, and warm hats. It was regarded as the simplest of the needle arts, and girls learned to knit before they attempted other, more complicated skills.

A woman absorbed in embroidery or crochet was a common sight in a middle-class home, and while there is no evidence that Cassatt practiced any form of needlework, it provided her with obvious inspiration. Lydia was her most frequent model, and her many depictions of Lydia knitting, sewing, or crocheting attest to her sister's skill. But Cassatt shows little interest in what Lydia makes. The striking feature of these works is her profound concentration.on what she is doing. Whatever the work, Lydia is totally, skillfully, and gracefully involved in her creative activity. Perhaps Cassatt saw in Lydia's absorption a counterpart to her own

Mrs. Robert S. Cassatt, the Artist's Mother
(c. 1889)

Although Katherine Kelso Cassatt's life followed the traditional path of marriage and motherhood, she taught her daughters to have a confidence in their own abilities that was ahead of their time. Louisine Havemeyer described her as "powerfully intelligent, executive and masterful and yet with that sense of duty and tender sympathy that she had transmitted to her daughter." Cassatt captures her true spirit in this oil: calm and self-possessed, her direct gaze reminds the viewer that she never hesitated to express her opinion Mother and daughter shared a close relationship until Mrs. Cassatt's death in 1895.

experience; in paintings such as *Lydia Crocheting in the Garden at Marly* (pages 24-5), Cassatt presents her sister as totally focused, sure of herself and not easily distracted from her work.

In all these images of solitary contentment—whether it be dressing, writing letters, reading or sewing—Cassatt restricts her vision to three settings: a modestly furnished bedroom, often no more than a washstand or a bureau and chair; a sun-filled parlor, with the details of the decor secondary to the flood of color and light; and a walled garden, fresh and bright with blooming flowers. In her choices, Cassatt reflects reality; these were the spaces in which a woman spent her day. While the garden has a long history as a symbol of female chastity in Renaissance art—the *hortus conclusus* of medieval and Renaissance painting that was the inviolable domain of the Virgin Mother—Cassatt's gardens express an essential modernity. In works such as *Lydia Crocheting in the Garden at Marly* at a summer villa, or *On the Balcony* outside a Paris apartment (page 34), the garden settings are painted from life, as vivid and immediate as the city garden Edith Wharton describes in the story *Madame de Treymes* (1906): "small, but intensely rich and deep—one of those wells of verdure and fragrance which everywhere sweeten the air of Paris by wafts blown above old walls on quiet streets."

Instead of being confining, the settings of Cassatt's paintings are always pleasant and, more importantly, private; they define a realm where a woman can spend her time alone, content with her own company and fulfilled in the richness of her experience.

Mary Cassatt

Social Life

A woman's social life revolved around a modest beverage. In the United States, Great Britain, and, to a lesser extent, France, affluent middle-class women would pay calls on one another to share a cup of tea. Whether a simple break in the day for conversation and refreshment, or a lavish entertainment designed by a hostess to impress her guests with her wealth and taste, the afternoon tea party was the main social ritual of the female world. Visits were brief, strict etiquette was followed, and conversation was limited to topics deemed acceptable. Within these boundaries, women conducted their friendships and exchanged their news. In the gilded age novels of Henry James and Edith Wharton, the tea party is often a formal and formidable affair. Here alliances are struck, marriages negotiated, and reputations lost or won. But in Cassatt's art, these gatherings are graced with an air of congeniality that brings to mind the genteel observation that opens James's

The Tea (c.1880)

In Britain and America, women entertained their guests with the ritual of afternoon tea. Visits were brief, just long enough to share a cup of tea and a cake, and exchange news about friends and family. As Cassatt shows here, callers did not remove their hats or gloves; keeping them on offered a polite indication of the intended brevity of the stay. In Paris Cassatt followed this Anglo-American custom, welcoming guests in her drawing room. The tea service in this painting, a family heirloom, made in 1813 for the artist's grandmother, suggests the elegance with which Cassatt entertained.

43

novel *Portrait of a Lady*: "There are few hours in life more agreeable than the hour dedicated to the ceremony known as afternoon tea."

Family was at the center of a woman's social network. Women cultivated close relationships not just with their siblings, but with sisters-in-law, cousins, and aunts. They also pursued friendships on the basis of shared experience or interest. The afternoon tea party might include women of varying ages and degrees of acquaintance. Out-of-town guests were expected to take part in their hostess's social engagements, to be present when callers were expected, and to accompany their hostess on her round of calls. These gatherings were almost exclusively female. When a man came to call, the nature of the event changed; he arrived alone in order to visit a specific party—a respected aunt or a fiancée's mother—rather than to join the group. Children were almost never present. When a girl joined her mother's social circle, it signaled her passage from the nursery into the world of women.

These afternoon gatherings were a familiar feature of Cassatt's life. Raised in a comfortable American household, she would undoubtedly have observed her mother entertaining guests. After her years of travel and study, when she first settled in Paris, Cassatt became the central figure in a lively group of highly intelligent American women who met at her house for tea and good conversation. When her parents arrived in Paris in 1877, they shaped their lives, as best they could, according to American habits, building a network of social contacts based on "At Homes," tea parties, and a love of horses. After their death, Cassatt was able to relax the rules if she wished. When it suited her, she followed convention to the letter, presiding in her home, as one journalist described, as "a rather prim, dignified, Philadelphia aristocrat." But, in her memoirs of Cassatt, Louisine Havemeyer recalls her as a generous—and often unorthodox—hostess, drawing great crowds of fascinating guests to her "delightful luncheons" and evening "At Homes." To Cassatt, her social circle was more important for its supportive friendships and its interesting exchange of ideas than for the status it might bring. The value she placed on female company is evident in her depictions of women meeting over a cup of tea.

Although a woman's social activities rarely began before the midday meal, she often spent hours in the morning preparing for them. Social correspondence demanded time and attention. According to Elizabeth Gaskell's *Compendium of Forms* (1882), invitations, acceptances, refusals, and announcements took the form of "notes." These were differentiated from letters by their brevity and formality. Gaskell recommends notes for "all matters of ceremony," ranging from afternoon engagements to weddings, as well as "communications between persons but slightly acquainted." Notes were written on heavy, good-quality paper; delicately tinted paper was permissible, but white was preferred. In this form of correspondence, a writer would refer to herself in the third person so no signature was necessary. Gaskell warns her readers to be consistent and not shift into personal pronouns: "Such a mistake would plainly indicate inexperience or carelessness." Wealthy women often hired a secretary to assist them with this type of correspondence. In Edith Wharton's *The House of Mirth* (1905), Lily Bart finds herself drafted to help her hostess with her letter-writing on a morning when the secretary is unavailable. Intent on maintaining her reputation as an amiable guest, Lily obliges. By ten in the morning, she is busy but bored in the drawing room, with "notes and dinner cards to write, lost addresses to hunt up, and other social drudgeries to perform."

A woman's wardrobe required much consideration, and a full social diary demanded an extensive one. All day dresses, whether plain or lavishly embellished, were referred to as morning gowns, the type of dress a woman would wear to receive her guests which Cassatt illustrates in the dry point and color print, *The Fitting* (page 46), in which a woman watches as a seamstress pins a hem in her simple new morning gown. Cassatt depicted a similar gown, with a pinafore-style bodice and long white sleeves, a second time, in *Afternoon Tea Party* (page 47) where it is worn by the hostess. Its simplicity stands in complete contrast to the garments worn by the visitor. A woman paying calls would choose a more elegant and elaborate morning gown with a matching hat and cloak, as well as gloves and a parasol. Books of etiquette advised women not to remove their cloaks, hats, or gloves during a call; no woman wanted her hostess to think that she planned to overstay her welcome.

Calls were always brief—fifteen to thirty minutes—and during most of the year, they were made in the afternoon between the hours of three and five. In late spring and summer, there was an extra hour allowed to take advantage of the extended daylight. Despite this strict convention, these were known as morning calls. The guide to etiquette in Gaskell's *Compendium of Forms* explains: "Fashion calls daylight morning, but before noon is too early for calling." Evening calls were less formal and longer in duration, but were reserved for close friends.

In some circles, a woman selected a specific day of the week to be "At Home." Casual acquaintances were expected to call only on the designated day; other afternoons were reserved for intimate friends. This restriction was waived for travelers in town for a brief stay who might not be able to call at the appropriate time. Gaskell warned women not to neglect or defy the practice, explaining: "All persons that move in society are governed by the laws of fashion, and calls of ceremony are part of the ordeal through which they must pass to social distinction." Only circumstances of "decrepitude" or "weakness" were allowed to excuse a woman from her calls.

Paying a call did not, however, always involve a visit. If the hostess was out or indisposed, the guest could leave a calling or visiting card. A proper card was made of substantial stock, printed—or preferably engraved—with the caller's name and address. A woman would carry her card case in her hand as she approached her hostess's house to ring the doorbell, and would pass a card or two to the

The Fitting (1891)

Even a modest social life required a woman to purchase and maintain an extensive wardrobe. A fitting at the dressmaker's was part of a woman's routine. Cassatt chose her subjects for the "Set of Ten" from these commonplace moments in a woman's life in response, perhaps, to the intimate glimpses of the feminine world portrayed in ukiyo-e *prints. Other elements—the raked perspective of the room and the blocks of pattern and tone—also suggest a Japanese influence. Using only a limited range of color and a delicate but confident line, Cassatt demonstrates a complete command of her medium.*

Afternoon Tea Party

(1890-1)

Cassatt introduces an element of dignity and reserve in this color print of two women at tea. Each woman's gesture is deliberate and restrained, giving an air of ceremony to the composition. The visitor's dark cape and plumed hat set her apart from her modestly dressed and obliging hostess. In an earlier version of the print, the guest was smiling, but in the final state, Cassatt gives her a more somber aspect. The print also features a rare touch of ornamental elegance: the gold rims on the cups and saucers that Cassatt painted by hand after the print was pulled.

servant who opened the door. A folded corner on the card indicated that the caller had others in her company. Very wealthy women often did not even leave their carriage to present their cards: their drivers would relieve them of that duty.

If the caller had no wish to enter, she simply asked that her card be delivered and would then leave. In many cases, such as a condolence call or an inquiry after the health of a new mother, no further contact was either expected or desired. Cards were also left in this manner to thank a hostess after a party or to inform a friend that the caller was going out of town. If the caller desired to see the woman of the house she waited while the servant went to inquire if she was in. If she was too busy, or felt unwell, or was simply not in the mood to receive guests, the servant would return with the message that the "lady was not at home." Cassatt often turned visitors away, declaring: "I have a right to refuse anyone, for I work from eight to ten hours a day." A caller would not be insulted by such a refusal, and as long as she

The Cup of Chocolate (1897)

At Cassatt's afternoon gatherings, the conversations were vibrant and intellectual, betraying a stronger affinity with the older French salon tradition than with the Anglo-American tea party characterized by small talk and gossip. In this lively pastel portrait, the young woman's erect posture, rapt gaze, and inquisitive expression suggest an intense level of exchange. Another French influence sets the image apart: the woman is drinking chocolate rather than the customary cup of tea. From her first years of residence in Paris, Cassatt freely mixed the social habits of her adopted country with those of her American origins.

left her card, she had fulfilled her social obligation.

A caller invited in for a visit knew exactly what to expect. Upon the servant's return, she would be escorted into the drawing room, typically located on the second floor. The hostess could express her special warmth by greeting her guest at the top of the stairs. With the exception of grand houses that featured separate "morning" rooms, in an average house or spacious apartment, the drawing room provided the setting for all women's social activities. The decor conformed to feminine preference, with light-colored walls or delicately printed wallpaper and a flower-patterned or India rug in the center of the room. Furnishings would include a large center table and comfortable couches and chairs arranged so as to be conducive to conversation.

The rooms Cassatt painted reflect her own taste as well as these conventions. In *The Tea* (pages 42-3), the rose and lavender striped wallpaper and the pink floral designs on the sofa lend lightness and warmth to a setting anchored by a heavy marble mantel surmounted by a gilt-framed mirror. Cassatt preferred her rooms filled with light, and in the print *Afternoon Tea Party* (page 47), the sun, filtered only by lace curtains as it floods the room, seems to dissolve the more solid forms of the furniture.

In many of these works, Cassatt included her own possessions, such as the porcelain vase on the mantel in *The Tea* and the decorative screen behind the caller in *Afternoon Tea Party*. May Alcott, sister of the novelist Louisa May Alcott, regularly called at Cassatt's home during her residence in Paris in 1876. She was struck by the sumptuous but tasteful decor and marveled at taking tea "while sitting in carved chairs, on Turkish rugs, with superb tapestries as backgrounds, and fine pictures on the wall looking down from their splendid frames." Plants and flowers also lent a decorative touch; in Cassatt's interiors painted at Marly-le-Roi in the summer of 1880, the presence of pots and vases of flowers seem to bring the garden indoors.

As soon as the callers had settled themselves comfortably, the hostess would serve the tea. A servant carried an urn of boiling water into the room, followed by the tea service on a tray. A tea service was often a treasured possession. Cassatt enjoyed using the silver set made for her grandmother Mary Stevenson in 1813; it appears on the table in *The Tea* (pages 42-3). The exquisite blue-and-white Canton china set featured in the portrait *Lady at the Tea Table* included a coffee service. It belonged to Cassatt's cousin Mrs. Robert Riddle, and when Cassatt admired it, Riddle gave it to her as a present. Cassatt hoped to express her gratitude by painting her cousin's portrait, but the honesty of the likeness displeased Mrs. Riddle. However, it is her imperious manner, rather than her plain face, that strikes the viewer. Her ringed fingers curl around the handle of the gold embellished porcelain pot with an air of possession, reminding the viewer that she was the original owner of this magnificent service.

With the tea service in place on the center table, the hostess would make the tea and then pour it out for her guests. The food served ranged from simple cakes and rolled slices of bread and butter to rich, sugary confections and dainty finger sandwiches. According to Alcott, Cassatt offered her guests sweet delicacies, "fluffy cream and chocolate, with French cakes." But tea parties were intended as a social call rather than an excuse for a meal, so guests exercised restraint, taking only a modest portion of what was offered and rarely more than one cup of tea. Women deliberately limited their tea consumption; it was regarded as a powerful stimulant.

If strictly followed, the rules of etiquette kept the conversation impersonal, and even superficial. Gaskell recommends only "the lighter topics of the day" and warns her readers that "religion, politics, and pedantic display are never in order on such occasions." But it is unlikely that these rules were universally obeyed. Callers came to exchange news, and this often took the form of gossip.

From all accounts, the conversation at Cassatt's gatherings rarely descended into gossip, and the tone was hardly superficial. Discussions of contemporary

Lady at the Tea Table (1883-5)
A stern, middle-aged woman, dressed in black, presides with formidable authority over a magnificent Canton tea service. The sitter, Cassatt's cousin Mrs. Robert Riddle, gave the artist the service, and Cassatt painted this portrait to thank her. But Riddle found the work unflattering and returned it. Katherine Cassatt had feared that her daughter's gift would not be well received by Riddle and her family, writing to her son Aleck that "they are not artistic people in their likes." Hurt by the rebuff, Cassatt hid the work in her own collection, but never doubted its quality. In later years she commented, "You may be sure it was like her."

Grandmother
Reading to Children

(1880)

During the summer of 1880, Cassatt and her family, including her brother Aleck, his wife, and their four children, rented a villa at Marly-le-Roi. In the country, life revolved around the family, and the children joined their aunt and grandmother as models for Cassatt's paintings. Here the three eldest children excitedly encircle their grandmother, who reads from a book of fairy tales. By placing her figures near a window to make the most of natural light, Cassatt manages to attain a sense of spontaneity.

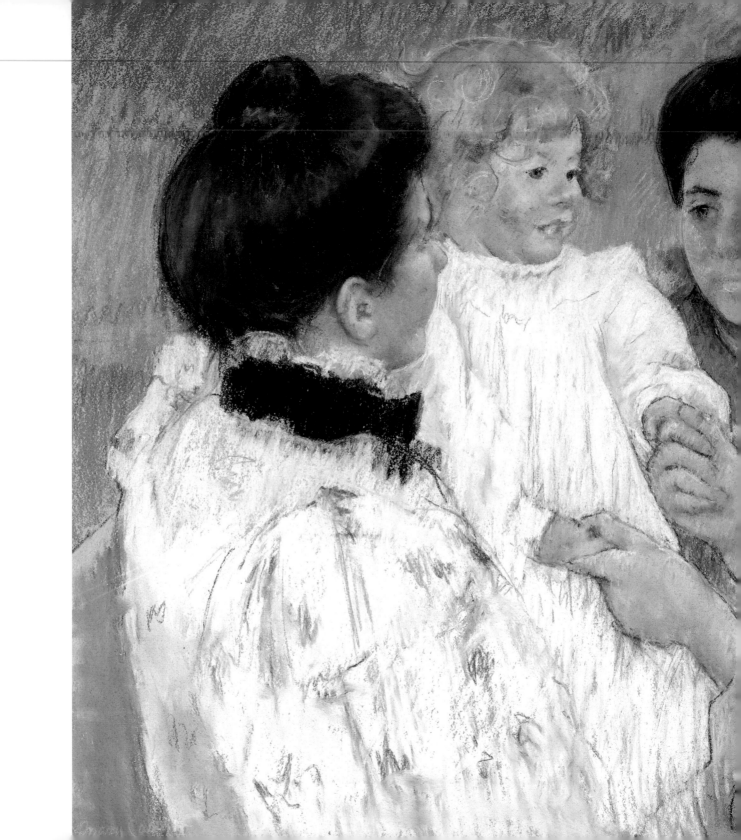

art and current literature no doubt led to lively debate. Cassatt loved to exchange ideas and challenge those of others, and she enjoyed surrounding herself with likeminded companions. Impressed with her intellectual insight and biting wit, May Alcott based a character on Cassatt in her novel *Diana and Persis* (1879); she appears as the central figure in a circle of independent-minded and outspoken women artists. In her art Cassatt uses a subtle device to suggest such a fascinating exchange. The women she portrays gathered around a tea table rarely speak. Instead, as seen in *The Tea* (pages 42-3) or *The Cup of Chocolate* (page 48), their eyes are directed to a point somewhere out of the picture plane. Still and attentive, their cups raised, these women are depicted as bright and avid listeners. It is the conversation, rather than the speaker, that attracts their attention.

In many of her later works, Cassatt portrays women brought together by their attention to a child. Although she had painted a few images of individual children in her early career, she did not bring them

Women Admiring a Child (1897)
In her later works, Cassatt featured children as the bond that brings women together. Here, a woman holds up her child to receive the loving attention of her friends. The mood is playful, and the child's expression signals her joy at being the focal point of the gathering. The rich tones and the short quick strokes of Cassatt's pastel work capture the natural immediacy of the moment; in the presence of the child, all formality dissolves. No rules of etiquette impede the delight these women share in amusing her.

into the adult circle until the summer of 1880. At that time, her brother Aleck, his wife Lois, and their four children Eddie, Katherine, Robbie, and Elsie, traveled from the United States to visit their family in France. Together, they rented a villa at Marly-le-Roi, where Cassatt, her parents, Lydia, and the children stayed while Aleck and Lois toured Europe. Away from the social obligations of the city, Cassatt's interest turned from friends to family. Now she found her subjects in the simple amusements offered to her nieces and nephews, such as reading aloud to them, as depicted in *Grandmother Reading to Children* (pages 52-3). After this visit by her nieces and nephews, the image of adults being attentive to children was firmly fixed in her repertoire. She maintained a close relationship with the children of both of her brothers, writing to them regularly and offering them warm hospitality whenever they visited her. In her later years, when her nieces visited her at Mesnil-Beaufresne, she took them for tea at Villotran, an eighteenth-century villa in the center of a beautiful park located about three miles (five kilometers) from her home. There, they were escorted through the gardens by the owners, the Mellons. Tea was taken in a garden gazebo in the form of a Venus temple and was brought to them on a donkey cart.

At the 1881 Impressionist exhibition, critic Joris Karl Huysmans was deeply touched by Cassatt's contribution, particularly by a painting of a woman holding a cup of tea. He discerned a special sensibility in her work, describing it as "a flutter of feminine nerves." But, even more striking to him was Cassatt's ability to express the quiet pleasures of a woman's social world. He described this as a "note of tenderness," something that differentiated her work from that of her French colleagues. "This indeed is the most characteristic quality of her talent, that Mlle. Cassatt, who, I believe, is an American, paints French women, but manages somehow to introduce into her Parisian interiors an 'at home' feeling. She has succeeded in expressing, as none of our own painters have managed to do, the joyful peace, the tranquil friendliness of the domestic interior."

In her art, as well as her own social circle, Cassatt tempered tradition with an open mind, an honest vision, and, on occasion, a willingness to challenge the rules. Little wonder that her images of the social lives of women are so inviting and congenial. She defined her subject according to her own values, and it is clear that to Cassatt, friendship and conversation meant far more than just the fulfillment of a social obligation.

Gathering Fruit (c. 1893)
Although Cassatt never returned to the allegorical mode of "The Modern Woman," painted for the Woman's Pavilion at the Columbian Exposition of 1893, she often returned to its figural ensembles. This drypoint and color print derives from the central panel, Young Women Plucking the Fruits of Knowledge, *but the symbolism of that work is here transformed into a modest genre scene. With delicate color washes setting the mood, this sunlit garden appears as a safe and happy haven. The baby, reaching for the freshly plucked grapes, is the center of the women's attention; his pleasure is all the diversion they desire on a sunny afternoon.*

Public Life

The sophisticated nineteenth-century city offered women a stimulating range of diversions beyond the confines of the drawing room. Elegant commercial avenues featured a new merchandising phenomenon—the department store. These tempted women with handsome displays in ground-floor windows, encouraging them to "window shop," then to enter and browse, and hopefully to make purchases on impulse. Women with cultural interests, however, preferred to visit museums or attend matinees of plays or concerts. Public parks, with their commodious paths and well-tended gardens, provided a woman with safe and pleasant places to stroll, and when she desired a break from her activities, there were tea rooms, with exclusively female clienteles, where she could relax and restore her energy with a beverage or light meal. Although governed by etiquette, when a woman ventured into the public arena, a wide range

In the Loge (1879)
Among the works of the Impressionists, few contemporary subjects expressed the vitality of modern public life as well as those set in the theater. Cassatt's interest in the motif was short-lived, corresponding exactly to the time when she and Degas were planning the themes for the journal Le Jour et La Nuit. *By confining her palette in this image to red, yellow, and brown, Cassatt simulates the rosy glow of artificial illumination in the dense texture of her pastel. The magnificent fan in the woman's hand was more than an accessory; it could be used to send a signal to another spectator or to hide her face from uninvited gazes.*

of pleasant possibilities unfolded before her.

As expressed in Edith Wharton's story *Madame de Treymes* (1906), late nineteenth-century Paris was unparalleled as a place for delightful diversion. As the tale opens, an American visitor, John Durham, admires a view of the Tuileries Gardens as he waits for his companion on the Rue de Rivoli. Compared to the "consummately ordered spectacle of Paris," his native New York City seems blighted with "unenlightened ugliness." Paris, he muses, must have "been boldly and deliberately planned as a background for the enjoyment of life." To a very great degree, Durham was correct. During the reign of Napoleon III (1852-70), the crooked streets and crumbling squares of central Paris had been replaced with broad, straight boulevards and grand gardens. The urban renovation, designed by Baron Georges Hausmann, sought to enhance the quality of public life. Both elegant and practical, Hausmann's plan was a success, and for decades to come Paris was to set the standard of beauty and accessibility in the modern city.

Paris also provided a seemingly limitless repertoire of lively subjects for contemporary art. At one time or another, every member of the Impressionist circle was inspired by the urban scene. In works such as *Le Pont de l'Europe* (1876) and *Rainy Day, Paris* (1877), Gustave Caillebotte celebrated the modernity of Parisian architecture and fashion. Pierre Auguste Renoir selected pleasure as his theme, painting the lively crowds in dance halls and beer gardens in pictures such as *Le Bal au Moulin de la Galette* (1876).

Edgar Degas surveyed the full range of urban experience, from family visits to public gardens—as in the *Place de la Concorde* (c. 1875)—to theatrical productions, including café-concerts as well as the ballet and the opera. Like her colleagues, Cassatt portrayed the vitality and diversity of Parisian life. But her interpretation was an individualistic and deliberately selective one, portraying Paris from an American woman's point of view.

Once Cassatt settled in Paris to pursue her career as a professional artist, she purged from her work everything that stood in the way of her portrayal of contemporary life. The romantic moodiness, ethnic costumes, and references to Old Master styles disappeared, to be replaced by an acutely observed record of the world around her. By concentrating on the subjects that reflected her own experience, she developed a natural honesty that made her work distinctive. It is notable that in these early works, she kept her vision focused on the domestic interior. Rather than being an indication of the lack of scope of her own life—although a single woman avoided appearing in public alone—this self-imposed selection allowed her to gain expertise in interpreting the subjects she knew best.

But identification with the Impressionists prompted Cassatt to look beyond the drawing room. By 1878, she began to carry a sketch book when she ventured out, in order to capture the images that flashed before her on the streets of Paris. In the following year, Degas's proposed journal *Le Jour et La Nuit* set itself the challenge of interpreting women's activities in the public domain, as well as their private lives. While the domestic interior provided the setting for one of Cassatt's etchings of this period—*The Visitor* (c. 1879-80), a careful study of a well-dressed caller rising from a chair in a drawing room—she also portrayed women at the opera. Two versions of *In the Opera Box* (c. 1879-80) record Cassatt's experimental approach: in one a bright light obscures the woman's features and in the other her face is cast in shadow. When the plans for Degas's journal failed, Katherine Cassatt blamed him for mismanaging the project and wasting her daughter's time: "Degas who is the leader undertook to get up a journal of etchings and got them all to work for it so that Mary had no time for painting." But, despite its failure, the endeavor had not only encouraged Cassatt to experiment with etching, it had directed her interest to those places where women appeared in the public arena, particularly those she frequented herself.

Cassatt loved the opera. In her youth in Philadelphia, she regularly attended musical performances, and while living in Parma, she took advantage of the opera productions by the local company. Opera was also a great attraction for her in Paris. The city boasted a lavish new hall, Charles Garnier's Paris Opéra, designed and built during the years 1861-74 as the crowning feature of Napoleon III's city plan. The magnificent façade, with its temple colonnade and the ebullient sculptures by Jean-Baptiste Carpeaux, prepared the patron for the grandeur of the spectacle within. The interior decor reveals that Garnier thought the experience of attending the opera should be as theatrical as the performance itself. Dominated by a grand staircase, the lobby provided a setting in which men and women paraded their most fashionable attire. For most patrons, being seen at the opera was of equal importance to what they saw on the stage.

Cassatt was clearly intrigued by the audience of the Paris Opéra. For a few years after the demise of *Le Jour et La Nuit*, the motif of the woman at the opera remained one of her favorites. But, her interpretation of this subject was not swayed by the spectacle of fashionable display. It was the spectators' act of observation that fascinated her. As early as 1878, she made on the spot sketches for the painting *In the Loge* (1879). The main figure is a modestly dressed woman in a black morning ensemble; rather than attending a grand evening at the opera, she is at a matinee. She is seated in the loge—the mezzanine-level balcony that runs directly above the boxes—and she appears to be alone, although it would have been improper to attend the opera without a companion. The performance, however, is not what holds her attention. Instead, she gazes through her opera glasses at a point directly across from her. In the distance, a man leans over the rail, also staring, perhaps at her. But the woman's somber costume and confident demeanor seems well able to deflect any unwanted gaze.

In her pictures, Cassatt ignored the pretentions of the patrons making grand entrances and displaying their finery as they stroll the promenade during the interval, but instead carefully observes fashion and etiquette. Costume distinguished between afternoon and evening performances. Like the woman in the oil, *In the Loge*, the sitter in the pastel *In the Loge* (pages 58-9) attends a matinee. Although her gown is colorful and decorative, its high neck extended with a lace insert and its long sleeves trimmed with ruffled cuffs mark it as a morning gown. Gloves and a fan were requisite accessories. The fan, however, had a practical use; as seen in this work, a woman could use it to shield her face from prying eyes.

Although guides to etiquette such as Gaskell's *Compendium* warned that "dress should always be consistent with one's age and natural exterior," most women wore revealing gowns for evening. Elegant evening ensembles gave them the opportunity for public display. An elaborate coiffure and magnificent jewelry would have enhanced the appearance of a mature woman, but the beauty of the young women in Cassatt's painting *The Loge* (page 65) requires no such artifice. Their gowns are fashionably cut, with the decolletage baring their shoulders and with long gloves covering their arms to the elbow. The woman on the right—identified as the daughter of Cassatt's friend, the poet Stéphane Mallarmé—wears a black velvet ribbon around her neck; this is more appropriate to her age than a gemstone necklace. The bouquet in her lap is another reference to her youth; it may also be a tribute from an admirer. In the novel *The Age of Innocence* (1920), Edith Wharton describes May Welland in similar attire at the opera. Her fiancé's admiring gaze embarrasses her, causing her to blush from the roots of her hair to "the young slope of her breast to the line where it met a modest tulle tucker fastened with a single gardenia." May directs her own eyes to the immense bunch of lilies of the valley on her lap, a gift from her future husband who interprets her nervous touching of the petals as an acknowledgment of his attentions. The young women in Cassatt's painting are equally shy. Mary Ellison, the woman on the left, crosses her arms protectively in front of her and retreats behind her fan. Unlike the eager young woman in Renoir's *First Outing* (1875-6), who leans forward, barely able to contain her excitement, these young women are self-conscious, intimidated by the unfamiliar—and perhaps overwhelming—surroundings.

Cassatt's careful attention to the details of costume reveals another of her passions. As Degas so clearly captured in his various studies of her and her sister at the Louvre for *Le Jour et La Nuit*, Cassatt dressed with distinction and flair. She painted her own

In the Loge (1879)
In nineteenth-century urban life, the opera house was a place to be seen as well as to enjoy the performance. In this intriguing and complex composition, Cassatt presents a middle-aged woman peering through her binoculars at a point well above the stage. Her high-necked gown indicates that she is at a matinee; gloves and a fan complete her ensemble. Further along the loge, out of the woman's range of view, a man leans over the rail to gaze, perhaps at her. But it would be a mistake to take this image as an anecdote. In its complex sight lines, along with the strongly focused foreground figure contrasting with the blurred forms on the periphery, this painting emulates the act of looking around at an audience.

portrait twice, in 1878 and again in 1880, and in each, the elegance of her ensemble is striking. Although she rarely referred to shopping in her letters, in two pastels of 1882, Degas portrays her as a delighted customer in a milliner's shop, trying on hats and inspecting the effect in a mirror.

It is unknown whether she frequented the new department stores of Paris; she seemed to prefer the couture houses, particularly those of Worth and Paquin. When her sisters-in-law visited, she advised them on a couturier, and was even known to buy costumes for her models at Paquin's sales, to ensure that they appeared elegant and modern in her work. Even late in life, Cassatt exhibited impeccable taste. When William Ivins, curator of prints at the Metropolitan Museum of Art, met her, he noted that she "dressed extremely well in a tailored manner," favoring "big hats with plumes" and "long amethyst chains with a lorgnette." Her clothing was made in Paris, according to Ivins, but she preferred English shoes, believing them to be more practical.

As in all aspects of a woman's life, clothing was subject to strict rules of decorum. All books of etiquette included a section on dress. Gaskell, for example, explains that good character may be more important than fine appearance, but first impressions are "apt to be permanent." She encourages women to dress with this in mind: "Many have owed their elevation to their attention to their toilet. Place, fortune, marriage, have all been lost by it." American women admired Parisian design, and those who could afford it made the journey to Paris once a year to replenish their wardrobes. Others had their measurements on file at Parisian couturiers, and the dresses were sent to them. Even less affluent American women tried to save enough to purchase a trousseau from France for their daughters. But Parisian fashion was often considered too radical for American tastes. After a shopping trip abroad, some women put their new wardrobes in storage, to be worn a season or two in the future. In *The Age of Innocence*, Wharton describes a Boston matron, who had a standing order with Worth for twelve dresses a year: two each of velvet, satin, and silk and six of poplin and cashmere. Near the end of her life, illness confined her for two years. At her death, her daughters discovered a bounty of "forty-eight Worth dresses that had never been taken out of the tissue paper, and when the girls left off their mourning they were able to wear the first lot at the Symphony concerts without looking in advance

The Loge (c.1882)
A young woman's first evening at the opera marked her passage into public society. Pierre Auguste Renoir's First Outing *was a tender rendition of this subject and Edith Wharton described it in her novel* The Age of Innocence. *The two young women here seem apprehensive and self-conscious in these unfamiliar surroundings. But, with their reserved gestures, they are faultlessly demure. The decolletage and cap sleeves of their gowns, as well as their elbow-length gloves, characterized all women's evening wear, but the simple velvet ribbon that encircles the neck of the girl on the right was a sign of her youth; mature women would have worn elaborate jewelry.*

LEFT Portrait of a Young Woman in Black (1883)

This portrait of the artist's sister-in-law Jennie Cassatt offers a study in contrasts. Although seated on a sofa in Cassatt's drawing room, Jennie is dressed to appear in public. Every item she wears is black, from the hat trimmed with feathers arranged in the form of wings, to the little beaded reticule in her gloved hands, revealing that the portrait was painted during the period of mourning for Lydia Cassatt. But the image conveys vitality rather than grief; behind the filmy veil, Jennie's face is radiant, and her surroundings, predominantly in shades of rose, set off the bright tint of her lips.

RIGHT Portrait of an Elderly Lady (c.1887)

The sitter in this portrait has never been identified, but her demeanor suggests an engaging personality. Her dark-toned garments are those of an older woman. While this may indicate that she is a widow, most elderly women selected somber colors for the city, wearing ivory or white only during the warmest days of summer. In contrast, the bunch of bright flowers on the woman's hat gives her a jaunty air.

of the fashion." At another point in the story, Newland Archer is struck by his wife May's insistence on wearing a sky-blue full-length cloak trimmed with swansdown out in the grime of London's streets. He marveled at "the religious reverence of even the most unworldly American women for the social advantage of dress," realizing "It's their armor."

Getting around the city could be fraught with difficulty for a woman. She might select from a number of options. There were carriages for hire, but it was preferable that a man, rather than a woman flag the driver's attention. A wealthy household would keep its own carriage and pony, often retaining the services of a driver and groom. When Cassatt's brother Aleck was promoted to the presidency of the Pennsylvania Railroad, he shared his good fortune by setting up a trust fund for his parents in 1879. They drew upon it to purchase a pony and carriage, and in *Woman and Child Driving* Cassatt painted her sister Lydia driving it in the Bois

Woman and Child Driving (1881)
Although Cassatt's association with the Impressionists led her to paint outdoors, landscape settings remained rare in her work. Even in this oil the specific location—the Bois de Boulogne—recedes in soft tones and indistinct forms behind the solidly rendered and brightly painted figures. Sitting nervously erect, Lydia Cassatt holds the reins of the family pony cart; Degas's niece sits beside her, and a young groom occupies the backward-facing seat. Each figure seems isolated from the other, suggesting the tense, self-conscious spirit often present in Degas's urban scenes.

de Boulogne with Degas's niece Odilie Fèvre at her side. The drive is purely for pleasure; to return home, the groom seated behind them would be expected to take over the reins. Another transportation option for women was the city omnibus, used by women of all classes. Some of these vehicles had seats located on an upper deck, so women were careful to check that the stairway was equipped with a "modesty panel" so that no one saw their legs as they made their ascent.

When Cassatt portrayed women out in the city with their children, she often positioned them so as to suggest their private realm within a public space. The group of figures in the print *In The Omnibus* (page 72) sit close to one another; Cassatt originally considered placing other figures to one side, but in the end preferred not to disturb the integrity of the ensemble. But, there is the sense that there are other passengers in the car; the observer sits on the opposite bench, precisely where Cassatt would have had to sit in order to draw.

Family groups that feature a father are rare in Cassatt's art. This might be attributed to the absence of male models of a particular age among her circle and to the fact that her sisters-in-law visited more often and for longer periods than their husbands, whose time to travel was often curtailed by the demands of their professions. But this absence may also be due to Cassatt's preference for portraying contemporary life as her own personal experience, strictly from a woman's viewpoint. *The Boating Party* (pages 74-5) may represent an exception. Cassatt painted the work at Cap d'Antibes on the Mediterranean where she and her mother had rented a winter retreat during the first months of 1894. The man and woman in the boat were hired models, but their relationship in the painting is ambiguous. The man at the oars wears the dark garments, broad cummerbund, and black beret associated with Provençal fishermen. He might represent a hired boatman, but the subtle play of glances between him and his passengers suggests a more intimate relationship.

Although Cassatt found a great variety of subjects within the home, her selection of motifs of women's public lives was limited. The opera audience held her interest only for a few years, and her depictions of women with their children in public parks are far outnumbered by those she placed in private gardens. The fashionable women in her portraits are ready to appear in the Paris streets, cafes, and galleries, but she chose to paint them in domestic interiors. And even when a group of women appear in a boat or on

Summertime (c.1894)
Several months after she purchased Château Mesnil-Beaufresne, Cassatt wrote "I am now painting with my models in the boat and I sit on the edge of the water and in these warm still September days it is lovely." The oil painting Summertime *reveals Cassatt's response to the delightful atmosphere she describes. Sunlight shimmers on the pale garments worn by the woman and the girl. Using rich tones and short brushstrokes, Cassatt also captures the sparkle of light on water, bringing to mind the masterful effects in the work of Claude Monet.*

Mary Cassatt

LEFT **In the Omnibus** (c.1891)

An elegant young mother, an extravagantly dressed baby,
and an attentive nursemaid sit close together in an omnibus
car, creating a private realm in a public space. In her
original drawing for the print, Cassatt depicted a man
seated on the mother's right; she then lightly superimposed
on him a standing woman. In the printed version both these
figures are absent, but the women and the child do not
appear to be alone in the car. The viewer occupies a
position on the opposite bench, and like the young mother,
catches a glimpse of the Seine as the bus crosses a bridge.

ABOVE **Feeding the Ducks** (c. 1894)

Cassatt often rendered similar subjects and compositions
in different media, to test the resulting effects of form and
color. Feeding the Ducks *shares the setting and*
atmospheric concerns of the painting Summertime*.*
The greater precision of the drypoint line, however, shifts
the emphasis from the sensual effect of light on water to
the anecdotal interest of the figures' actions. The
decorative patterns on the women's garments relate this
print to the aesthetic concerns of the prints in the
"Set of Ten."

an omnibus, their privacy is never violated by intruders or accidental interruptions.

In her own life, Cassatt did not choose isolation. She regularly attended exhibitions, dinner parties, and the theater. Louisine Havemeyer recalled her lamenting "I give myself out too much," but she admired her friend's energy: "I have seen her entertain a huge house party until two in the morning and be ready for another busy day after only a few hours rest." Cassatt's selectivity in her interpretation of public life was intentional, and was shaped by the attitudes of her generation. The domestic interior was a woman's realm. In public, she was constantly on display, but in the privacy of her home or among friends, she was freer to follow her own inclinations. Disdaining artifice in all aspects of life, Cassatt always sought natural and spontaneous subjects for her art. The result was that she preferred to place her sitters in private places, where their actions and demeanor would be unencumbered by public scrutiny.

The Boating Party (1893-4)
In the early months of 1894, Cassatt and her mother stayed at Cap d'Antibes. Cassatt took advantage of the picturesque setting to paint The Boating Party. *With its broad flat planes of strong color, the composition reveals Cassatt's continuing interest in the Japanese aesthetic. Dressed in muted tones, the mother and her squirming child strike a contrast with the dark silhouette of the boatman. The figures are united by the thick yellow brushstrokes of the boat, as well as by a subtle exchange of glances.*

Motherhood

The mother—devoted, nurturing, and wise—was the central icon of nineteenth-century womanhood. Throughout their youth, girls were taught that they were destined for matrimony, not just for the love or security it would provide, but for the opportunity to bear and rear children. The role of motherhood defined women; the qualities associated with being a good mother were regarded as instinctively feminine. And, the rewards of motherhood were expected to be fulfilling; healthy, obedient, and accomplished children were the measure of a woman's worth. Every voice of nineteenth-century culture—poetry, literature, popular journalism—promoted this ideal. Women were urged to model themselves on such examples of selfless devotion as Marmee, the sensible mother in Louisa May Alcott's *Little Women* (1868). Cold or self-centered mothers, such as the harsh and distant Mrs. Touchett in Henry James's *Portrait of a Lady* (1881) or the feckless mother in his *Daisy Miller* (1881),

Breakfast in Bed (1897)
In this oil, Cassatt portrays a modest pleasure shared by a mother and child. In a loving embrace, the mother encircles her lively child, brought to her bed upon awaking. Breakfast—a cup of chocolate and some biscuits—rests on a stand at her bedside. Cassatt captures the delicacy of the morning light with a subtle palette, ranging from the dull gray-green of the night table to the rosy cheeks of the child. Cassatt's niece Ellen Mary posed for this image, and the contrast between her pert energy and the mother's languid ease heightens the sense of the passing moment.

were blamed for spoiling the lives of their children. Although Cassatt never married or raised a child, she placed great value on the experience of motherhood. "After all," she observed, "a woman's vocation in life is to bear children."

The idealization of motherhood had long influenced the portrayal of the mother and child in the visual arts. European tradition overlaid the image with sacred connotations; since the Renaissance, the portrayal of the Madonna and the Christ child represented the essential humanity of the divine. In nineteenth-century Europe and America, the mother-and-child dyad became a secular icon, reflecting contemporary reverence for motherhood and family. Few subjects enjoyed as wide a popularity in the arts of the day. It was a favorite of American anecdotal painters, such as Lily Martin Spencer and Thomas Hovenden, who often loaded their depictions with cloying sentimentality. It was also interpreted by many Impressionists; Pierre Auguste Renoir and Berthe Morisot endowed their mother-and-child images with special serenity and grace. It was a theme that influential and unconventional artists—ranging from Puvis de Chavannes and Eugène Carrière to Paul Gauguin and Vincent van Gogh—explored, bringing it to the attention of a large and varied audience. And the subject of mother and child was to shape Cassatt's reputation. She was so closely linked with the depiction of motherhood that her first biography, written by Achille Segard in 1913, bore the title *Cassatt: Un Peintre des enfants et des mères*.

One distinctive quality set Cassatt's maternal subjects apart from those of her contemporaries, and that was their fidelity to life. Critics recognized this, some attributing it to the fact that Cassatt was a woman, others expressing surprise that she could interpret the subject so well without personal experience. Still others—notably American critics—lamented her lack of sentimentality. But those familiar with the full range of her art realized that this genuine spirit came from years of careful and keen observation of women's lives.

The social changes that had resulted in the separation of the activities of men and women, confining women mostly to the domestic sphere, prompted writers concerned with women's issues to evaluate the situation. Harriet Beecher Stowe and Catherine Beecher both urged women to regard their obligations to family and household as their destiny. In *The American Woman's Home* (1869), they defined "woman's mission" as one of "self-denial" and "self-sacrificing labors." A woman's children were the worthiest beneficiaries of her selflessness. In expressing these opinions, Stowe and Beecher were advocating a female identity that came to be known as the "True Woman." A True Woman instinctively understood her domestic duties and gained her deepest personal fulfillment through them. She was an endless source of care and comfort for her children and the guardian of their moral character. Warmth and wisdom were part of her nature, and love was the basis for all her actions. This image of maternity was promoted in household manuals, women's journals, and home magazines. Aphorisms, such as social reformer Amos Bronson Alcott's "The mother's heart is the child's schoolroom," and writer William Goldsmith Brown's "The sweetest sound to mortals given are heard in Mother, Home, and Heaven," made the new ideal seem like well-worn folk wisdom. In literature, Louisa May Alcott's Marmee was the most perfect incarnation of the True Woman.

This new emphasis on the role of the mother also redefined the role of the child. In the United States, during colonial times and the early years of nationhood, children were regarded, at best, as extra hands for work and, at worst, as extra mouths to feed. As head of the household, a father exerted the strictest parental authority and practiced harsh child rearing methods, including whippings for "Old Adam's sake."

By the middle of the nineteenth century, most parental duties had passed from men to women. Gentler methods of child rearing, based on Jean Jacques Rousseau's theories of nurture over discipline, were promoted by social activists such as Ralph Waldo Emerson, Henry David Thoreau, and Henry Ward Beecher. Children were now seen as innocent and helpless, requiring the guidance of a loving mother as much as food and shelter. Emerson once recalled that a friend regretted having been born "when childhood was nothing" and having to endure his maturity "when childhood was everything."

But in most middle-class and affluent households, the reality fell far short of the ideal. Women, for the most part, spent little time on child care. The daily needs of children were handled by the household staff, which might include a children's nurse or "nanny." Most of the child's time was spent in the day nursery, usually located at the top of the house, far away from the drawing room. Children ate their meals there as well; the large meal after church on Sunday was the only one regularly shared by the whole family. Devoted mothers made a point of visiting their children in the nursery when they had their tea, which served as their evening meal before bedtime.

Manuals of etiquette were constantly spelling out the restrictions to be imposed on children. They should not be taken along on calls. They should be taught not to bother adults and not to speak unless asked a question. Gaskell's *Compendium of Forms* (1882) urged mothers to separate their maternal duties from their social life: "Never allow your own children in the drawing-room when you receive, nor take them to walk or drive with your friends, nor spend the day in adult company, if you value their happiness." While these restrictions seem harsh and in conflict with the prevailing ideal of selfless mothering, they clearly defined the time shared by mother and child as separate from social or public obligations. Although in individual households, mothers spent as little or as much time with their children as they were inclined, one factor remained consistent: that time was to be protected and private—an intimate shared moment.

Never having children of her own, Cassatt was able to view motherhood with some objectivity. Her sense of her own worth was not based on romanticized contemporary ideals and she refused to judge other women by such unrealistic standards. As she observed mothers with their children and women engaged in child care, she looked instead for the same qualities she valued in every aspect of life—competence and concentration, grace and sympathy.

The circumstances that brought the image of women and children into her repertoire were also out of the ordinary. Although she painted a few pictures featuring children during her first years in Paris, the subject did not emerge consistently in her art until the summer of 1880 when her brother Aleck and his family came to visit from the United States. While Aleck and his wife Lois toured Europe, their four children stayed at Marly-le-Roi with their grandparents and their aunts. Away from their normal social obligations, the adults were able to lavish attention on the children. Cassatt painted what she observed—her mother reading to them or a nurse washing them before bedtime. It was not until a later visit, this time by her brother Gardner, with his wife Jennie and their infant son, that the image of maternal devotion found a firm place in her repertoire. Sometime in January 1888, Cassatt used Jennie and little Gardner as models for a drypoint print. It was a simple rendition of Jennie holding her child, giving him her full attention. As so often with subjects that interested her, Cassatt began to explore the possible variations on the motif, by using different media, by making compositional changes, and by capturing the subtle nuances of expression.

But Cassatt's models were not always women with their own children. In addition to having family and household members pose for her, she hired professionals. She paired the women and children to attain the effect she wanted, looking for a natural sympathy to the child on the part of the woman and a comfortable ease with the woman on the part of the child. The poses she selected engaged them with one another and stimulated their natural responses. In *Mother About to Wash her Sleepy Child*, the woman's firm embrace keeps the child safe and secure, allowing her to surrender to sleep. Other subjects prompt the woman to respond to the baby, whispering reassurance as in *Agatha and Her Child* (page 82) or giving comfort in the form of a kiss, as in *Young Thomas and his Mother* (page 83). Cassatt was a careful observer of children's natural behavior, catching their random gestures and unpredictable expressions with great authenticity. The children she depicts fidget, and snuggle, and stare, just as they would in reality.

Thus for an era that romanticized motherhood and children, Cassatt's paintings display remarkable honesty. It was standard to portray mothers as serenely beautiful Madonnas with angelic infants—an image calculated to confirm the ideal and charm the viewer. However, in a review of the Impressionist exhibition of 1881, Joris-Karl Huysmans expressed his exasperation with the conventional image of maternity: "Oh, my God! those babies! How those portraits have made my flesh crawl, time and again!—A whole passel of English and French smearers have painted them in such stupid and pretentious poses!"

**Mother About to Wash her
Sleepy Child** (c.1880)
*Cassatt achieved a sense of
spontaneity in her work by carefully
observing her models and recording
their natural gestures. For the subject
of this oil, she undertook a daring
challenge: to capture the random
movements of a sleepy child in a
woman's lap. In this early example
of a picture of a woman absorbed
in caring for a child—perhaps
inspired by the visit of her nieces
and nephews in 1880—Cassatt
uses the woman's solid form to
suggest security and stability. Safe in
her embrace, the child relaxes into a
lazy sprawl and surrenders to sleep.*

MOTHERHOOD 82

To his delight, Cassatt offered an alternative: "The gallery in which her canvases hang contains a mother reading, surrounded by tykes, and another mother kissing her baby on the cheeks—they are irreproachable, softly lustrous pearls; they are family life painted with distinction, with love. "

About a decade later, in 1892 when Cassatt was deeply involved with her explorations of the mother-and-child motif, the critic Georges Lecomte applauded her "infinitely human and loving mothers who clasp to their bosom pink-skinned babies who are well and truly alive and have no thought for anything but their mother's caresses." But, many of Cassatt's contemporaries were not ready for the blunt sincerity and absence of polished prettiness in her interpretation of their favorite subject. Cassatt's dealer Paul Durand-Ruel made her work appear more conventional than it was by describing her subject as "la sainte famille moderne." Other critics picked up this association: Lecomte also described her work as that of an artist of the modern Holy Family, and in the February

LEFT **Agatha and Her Child** (1892)
Cassatt often selected pastel as the medium for her depiction of children. The dense, velvet-like surface left by chalk on the paper suggests the fine texture of a baby's skin. In this work, Cassatt also used color to evoke a mood of intimacy. Against a background of short blunt strokes in delicate shades of buff, gray, and blue, Cassatt works the figures in richer hues of similar tones. The warm salmon pink of the baby's dress is repeated in his lips, while his shining bright eyes reflect the blue of his mother's gown.

ABOVE **Young Thomas and His Mother** (1893)
As a determined modernist, Cassatt avoided sentimentality. When this pastel was shown in the United States in 1895, one reviewer called it "hard" and "inharmonious." Yet the gentle gesture of the mother expresses a universal maternal compassion. An image such as this could have easily declined into anecdote, but Cassatt withholds the source of little Thomas's discontent from the viewer. Mother and son share the emotional moment; the viewer, like Cassatt, can only observe.

LEFT **Mother and Child** (c.1890)

Although after 1880, children appear regularly in Cassatt's work, the focused theme of maternal devotion came later. A drypoint print of her sister-in-law Jennie holding her son Gardner, inscribed "Jan/88," may be the first example. This oil, painted two years later, combines elements of her earlier work with her new interest. The setting has the cozy domestic air of her solitary and social subjects, while the baby's relaxed posture recalls the theme of the sleepy child of the previous decade. But the complex intertwining of her models' hands and arms, as well as the woman's selfless expression, point to Cassatt's mature renditions of the motif.

ABOVE **Susan Comforting the Baby** (c.1881)

In a sunlit garden, Cassatt's maid Susan attends to a baby in a carriage. The child is utterly distraught; with one hand she holds her head, while with the other she firmly grasps Susan's wrist. Her facial expression—eyebrows elevated, eyes wide in bewilderment, lips pouting, ready to open in a wail—elicits amusement, but is completely natural; it is the artless response of an upset child. The critic Georges Lecomte praised Cassatt for her natural presentation of children's gestures and expressions in all their awkwardness and simplicity. Never bowing to "conventional prettiness," Cassatt rendered children "true to life."

issue of *Good Housekeeping Magazine* in 1910, Gardner Teall characterized her as a "true and gifted humanist," for her modern and American response to the Old Master tradition of the mother and child. But, some Americans decried the lack of sentiment in her work, finding her modern imagery "hard" and "inharmonious," and clearly at odds with their expectations of her.

In Cassatt's day, it was widely believed that a woman artist could bring a particular empathy to the subject of mother and child because her instincts were maternal. Huysmans, for instance, saw in Cassatt's work an essential feeling that "a man could not render." "Only a woman," he claimed, "can pose a child, dress it, put in pins without sticking herself." Cassatt agreed that particular elements distinguished a woman's art— "the sweetness of childhood, the charm of womanhood"—and she asserted "If I have not been absolutely feminine, then I have failed." But, what Cassatt meant by "feminine" differed from Huysmans' understanding of the term. For Cassatt, it was not her ability as a woman to care for a child, but her identity as a woman artist that enabled her to portray these subjects from a woman's point of view.

Aside from the honesty of her vision and the natural appearance of her models, Cassatt's maternal imagery is distinctive on two remarkable counts: her ability to evoke an aura of privacy and her portrayal of the trust between mother and child. Her long involvement with the domestic setting—as well as the importance she gives to a woman's sense of self—

Mother Combing her Child's Hair (c.1901)
This oil was one of the first works Cassatt completed after her return to Paris from the United States in 1898. It marks a new phase in her depiction of maternal subjects, featuring older children—mostly girls—with their mothers, engaged in the routine activities of daily life. But, the painting also continues Cassatt's explorations in compositional complexity. As in Reading Le Figaro *(page 33), Cassatt places a mirror to the woman's right to counterpoise figure and reflection. The rich, vivid surface results from combining media—pastel and gouache—with contour lines added for emphasis around the hands of the figures.*

The Child's Bath
(1893)

In this intimate glimpse of a woman bathing a child, the degree to which Cassatt captures her sitters' mutual absorption is unparalleled. Woman and child seem to exist as a single entity. They gaze in the same direction, and their features mirror one another. The child echoes her mother's gestures; the woman braces the child at the waist, while the child braces herself on her mother's knee. The woman's hand tenderly encircles the child's right foot, while the child's hand curls around her own thigh. To heighten the sense of intimacy, Cassatt chose a high viewpoint, placing the spectator at a protective distance.

Maternal Caress
(1890-1)

The subjects portrayed in Cassatt's print suite the "Set of Ten" present a loose sequence of events in a woman's day. Here, a woman shares a loving moment with her child. Japanese influence is particularly strong in this print. The low, forward placement of the main figures, the flattened perspective of the room, and the contrast of decorative patterns all contribute to an atmosphere of enclosure and privacy.

endow her with a special understanding of the atmosphere of private spaces. Some of the aesthetic devices she uses to convey a feeling of safety and enclosure were inspired by the compositional arrangements of *ukiyo-e* prints. As in the print *Maternal Caress* (page 89), Cassatt moves her figure forward to the edge of the picture plane. The use of a raked perspective causes the floor behind the mother to rise sharply, limiting the feeling of space. The figure embracing her child is seen as if the viewer is looking down from another plane. It is possible to look into the space, but there is no way to enter. Cassatt used a similar configuration for one of her most intimate maternal expressions, *The Child's Bath* (page 88). In both works, she defines the realm of the mother and child as personal and private.

Cassatt portrayed a mother's love and a child's trust through their touching one another. Some of the gestures she depicts are fleeting—the mother's lips moving against her baby's cheek in *Agatha and her Child* (page 82)—while others—as in *Young Thomas and his Mother* (page 83)—are quite deliberate. The gentility of purposeful touch—as in *The Child's Bath*—conveys a woman's genuine absorption in the routine acts of nurture and care. The tender exchange of caresses in *Mother Jeanne Nursing her Baby* (half-title page), draws the woman and child into a secure and loving bond of mutual satisfaction. Bound for a moment in contentment and trust, mother and child seem as one.

In all of these images, mother and child exist in their own time and space. No one can intrude or participate in their loving, intimate exchange. They share an intimate bond that is exclusive to a woman's experience. But, as depicted in the curious outward gaze of the girl in *Young Mother Sewing*, Cassatt recognized that as children grow they seek out more in life than their mother's attentions. This mother, like so many of Cassatt's women, gives herself fully to the task at hand, without thinking of the future. For throughout Cassatt's art, women find tranquility and satisfaction in occupations of many sorts, whether it be reading, sewing, conversing, or caring for a child. That was Cassatt's own experience and that was what she saw in her observations of women's lives.

RIGHT **Young Mother Sewing** (c.1900)
Cassatt reworks some of the most enduring elements of her art in this charming painting. The striking self-absorption of the mother recalls Cassatt's keen observation of women in solitary activity. Behind the mother, the bright view out of the window is reminiscent of her Impressionist experiments in plein air *painting, while the broad, simple divisions of the background space reveal her assimilation of the Japanese aesthetic. But Cassatt breaks with her usual technique of maintaining a reserved distance from her subjects; with unprecedented boldness, the little girl levels her gaze directly at the viewer.*

OVERLEAF **Mother and Child** (1900)
In society circles, children were rarely welcome, but as in this lively portrait, Cassatt depicted children as bright and responsive to the adults around them. While the baby's mother gazes serenely at their reflection in a mirror, the child looks around the room behind, as if eager for other distractions.

Author's Acknowledgments

When I was a child, my mother often took me to the Art Institute of Chicago. Our excursions varied, but one painting was always on our itinerary: Mary Cassatt's *The Child's Bath* (1893). I never realized then that it was my mother's favorite painting, but I always looked forward to seeing it. The painting made me wonder: Who was the mother? Do I look like the child? Wouldn't my mother look nice in a striped cotton dress? Familiarity with *The Child's Bath* taught me the pleasure of knowing a painting well and thinking about it long after leaving the museum.

It was with great pleasure, then, that I returned to the art of Mary Cassatt to write this book, and I would like to thank the people who made this endeavor possible.

For initiating the project and encouraging me with insight and understanding every step of the way, I thank my editor Caroline Bugler. I would like to thank Steven Parissien of the Paul Mellon Centre for British Studies for guiding me to her. I am also grateful to Hilary Mandleberg for editing the typescript and to Trish Going for the book design. My sincere gratitude also goes to Amy E. Henderson and Shelly Roman of the Terra Museum of American Art and Kristina Waldron of the Newberry Library for their valuable research assistance; to Kevin Sharp of the Art Institute of Chicago for his ready help; and to Judith A. Barter of the Art Institute of Chicago for her honesty and encouragement in the course of our discussions as I began my work. Most of all, I would like to thank my mother Elinor R. Mancoff. I can never look at Cassatt's paintings without thinking of her, and I dedicate this book to her on the occasion of her seventy-fifth birthday.

Selected Bibliography

Barter, Judith A., *Mary Cassatt: Modern Woman*. Chicago: Art Institute of Chicago, 1998.

Breeskin, Adelyn D., *Mary Cassatt: A Catalogue Raisonné of the Graphic Work*. Washington, DC: Smithsonian Institution Press, 1979.

Effeny, Alison, *Cassatt*. London: Studio Editions, 1991.

Havemeyer, Lousine, *Sixteen to Sixty: Memoirs of a Collector* (1930). New York: Ursus Press, 1993.

James, Henry, *Portrait of a Lady* (1881). New York: Knopf, 1991.

Lindsay, Suzanne, *Mary Cassatt and Philadelphia*. Philadelphia: Philadelphia Museum of Art, 1985.

Matthews, Nancy Mowll (ed.), *Cassatt and Her Circle: Selected Letters*. New York: Abbeville Press, 1984.

Matthews, Nancy Mowll (ed.), *Cassatt: A Retrospective*. Southport, Connecticut: Hugh Lauter Levin Associates, Inc., 1996.

Matthews, Nancy Mowll, *Mary Cassatt: A Life*. New York: Villard Books, 1994.

Mintz, Steven, *A Prison of Expectations: The Family in Victorian Culture*. New York: New York University Press, 1983.

Mitchell, Sally, *Daily Life in Victorian England*. Westport, Connecticut: Greenwood Press, 1996.

Rewald, John, *The History of Impressionism*. New York: Museum of Modern Art, 1973.

Segard, Achille, *Mary Cassatt: Un Peintre des enfants et des mères*. Paris: Librairie Paul Ollendorf, 1913.

Smith Rosenberg, Carroll, *Disorderly Conduct: Visions of Gender in Victorian America*. New York: Oxford University Press, 1985.

Wharton, Edith, *An Edith Wharton Treasury*. New York: Appleton-Century-Crofts, 1950.

Wharton Edith, *The House of Mirth* (1905). New York: MacMillan Publishing Co: 1987.

Publisher's Acknowledgments

Frances Lincoln Publishers would like to thank Helen Baz for supplying the index, and Maggi McCormick, Ruth Carim and Anne Askwith for their help with the book.

Project Editor Caroline Bugler
Editor Hilary Mandleberg
Editorial Assistant Tom Windross
Picture Researcher Sue Gladstone
Production Peter Hinton
Art Director Caroline Hillier
Editorial Director Erica Hunningher